Oh, So Cute!
Plastic Canvas™

Edited by Vicki Blizzard

Oh, So Cute!
Plastic Canvas

Editor: Vicki Blizzard
Art Director: Brad Snow
Publishing Services Manager: Brenda Gallmeyer

Associate Editor: Lisa M. Fosnaugh
Copy Supervisor: Michelle Beck
Copy Editors: Conor Allen, Mary O'Donnell, Beverly Richardson
Technical Editor: June Sprunger

Graphic Arts Supervisor: Ronda Bechinski
Book Design: Edith Teegarden
Graphic Artists: Jessi Butler, Vicki Staggs
Production Assistants: Cheryl Kempf, Marj Morgan

Photography: Justin P. Wiard, Kelly Wiard

Chief Executive Officer: John Robinson
Publishing Director: David McKee
Marketing Director: Dan Fink
Editorial Director: Vivian Rothe

Printed in China
First Printing: 2005

Library of Congress Control Number: 2004116593
Hardcover ISBN: 1-57367-198-3
Softcover ISBN: 1-57367-217-3

Every effort has been made to ensure the accuracy and completeness of the
instructions in this book. However, we cannot be responsible for human
error or for the results when using materials other than those specified in
the instructions, or for variations in individual work.

1 2 3 4 5 6 7 8 9

A Warm Welcome
From the Editor

Dear Readers,

I just love plastic canvas. I love the ease of stitching, I love the bright colors of yarn and I love adding layers of dimension. Most of all, I love hearing someone say, "Oh, that's so cute!" when I show them my finished projects.

We asked our favorite plastic canvas designers to send us projects that are cute and cheery, sure to induce warm smiles and happy expressions. We believe they have done just that, and we're thrilled to share them with you.

Our collection of ornaments, containers, wall hangings, shelf sitters and—everyone's favorite—tissue box covers are fun to create, fun to give and fun to display in your home.

Leaf through the pages of this book, and we know you'll be inspired often to stop and say, "That's so cute!" And you just won't be able to wait to start stitching!

Warm regards,

Vicki Blizzard

Contents

Precious Ornaments

Cute Containers

Whimsical Wall Hangings

I see the Moon
and the Moon sees me
God bless the Moon
and God bless me!

Darling Kitchen Decor

Sweet Sit-Arounds

Delightful Tissue Covers

Precious Ornaments

Add darling accents to your home this year with stitched ornaments for tree or mantel! Plastic canvas ornaments also make wonderful gifts.

Christmas in Ladybug Land

Add a touch of whimsy to your holiday decor with these charming little bugs who are busy decorating a tree! Designs by Kathleen Hurley

Skill Level
Beginner

Size
Right-Facing Ladybug: 3⅜ inches W x 6½ inches H (8.6cm x 16.5cm), excluding hanger

Left-Facing Ladybug (with star): 5½ inches W x 6¼ inches H (14cm x 15.9cm), excluding hanger

Christmas Tree: 3⅜ inches W x 3⅞ inches H (8.6cm x 9.8cm), excluding hanger

Materials
- 1 sheet 7-count plastic canvas
- Coats & Clark Red Heart Classic worsted weight yarn Art. E267 as listed in color key
- #16 tapestry needle
- 26 (8mm) multicolored round faceted acrylic beads
- White thread
- 1 yard (1m) gold cord
- Hot-glue gun

Instructions
1. Cut plastic canvas according to graphs.

2. Stitch and Overcast pieces following graphs, working uncoded areas on ladybugs with sea coral Continental Stitches and uncoded background on tree with paddy green Continental Stitches.

3. When background stitching is completed, use 2 plies yarn to work Backstitches and French Knots.

4. Using white thread, attach random colors of beads to tree where indicated on graph.

5. For hangers, cut three equal lengths of gold cord. Thread cord from back to front through holes indicated on ladybug and tree graphs. Tie ends together in a knot to form a loop for hanging.

6. Glue star to extended hand of left-facing ladybug. ✄

Star
7 holes x 7 holes
Cut 1

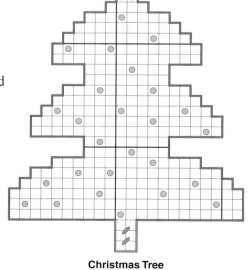

Christmas Tree
22 holes x 25 holes
Cut 1

COLOR KEY	
Yards	**Worsted Weight Yarn**
6 (5.5m)	☐ White #1
2 (1.9m)	■ Black #12
1 (1m)	☐ Yellow #230
1 (1m)	▨ Mid brown #339
7 (6.5m)	▨ Paddy green #686
1 (1m)	☐ Grenadine #730
5 (4.6m)	■ Cherry red #912
5 (4.6m)	Uncoded areas on ladybugs are sea coral #246 Continental Stitches
	Uncoded background on Christmas tree is paddy green #686 Continental Stitches
	⁄ Sea coral #246 Overcasting
	⁄ Black #12 (2-ply) Backstitch
	⁄ Cherry red #912 (2-ply) Backstitch
	● Black #12 (2-ply) French Knot
	● Cherry red #912 (2-ply) French Knot
	○ Attach bead
	○ Attach hanging cord
Color numbers given are for Coats & Clark Red Heart Classic worsted weight yarn Art. E267.	

Right-Facing Ladybug
22 holes x 42 holes
Cut 1

Left-Facing Ladybug
32 holes x 41 holes
Cut 1

Joy

Rejoice in the season with a cute little mouse swinging from a holiday wreath. Design by Judy Collishaw

Skill Level
Beginner

Size
5⅜ inches W x 5½ inches H (13.7cm x 14cm), excluding tail and hanger

Materials
- ½ sheet 7-count plastic canvas
- Worsted weight yarn as listed in color key
- #5 pearl cotton as listed in color key
- DMC 6-strand metallic embroidery floss as listed in color key
- #16 tapestry needle
- 6 inches/15.2cm metallic gold thread
- Hot-glue gun

Instructions

1. Cut plastic canvas according to graphs (this page and 13).

2. Stitch and Overcast pieces following graphs, working uncoded areas with white Continental Stitches.

3. When background stitching and Overcasting are completed, work Straight Stitch for nose on mouse head with 4 plies black yarn and French Knots on the wreath with 2 plies red.

4. Work pearl cotton backstitches and Straight Stitches on front paws and overalls. Use 2 strands (12 plies) gold embroidery floss to Backstitch buckles on overalls.

5. Using photo as a guide throughout assembly, glue back paws to bottom front of body. Glue top edge of body behind bottom edge of wreath. Glue head and front paws to front of wreath.

6. Cut a 2-inch length of gray yarn and glue to bottom back of mouse body for tail.

7. For hanger, tie ends of metallic gold thread together in a knot to form a loop. Glue knot to top center back of wreath. ✂

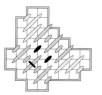

Mouse Head
8 holes x 8 holes
Cut 1

Mouse Back Paw
4 holes x 4 holes
Cut 2

Mouse Front Paw
4 holes x 4 holes
Cut 2

Graphs continued on page 13

Water Babies

These friendly sea creatures will frolic their way into your heart with their charming holiday gifts! Designs by Nancy Knapp

Skill Level
Beginner

Size
Christmas Seal (with wreath): 4⅜ inches W x 4¼ inches H (11.1cm x 10.8cm), excluding hanger

Otter (with gift): 5 inches W x 3⅜ inches H (12.7cm x 8.6cm), excluding hanger

Walrus: 6 inches W x 2½ inches H (15.2cm x 6.4cm), excluding hanger

Materials
Each Ornament
- ⅔ sheet 7-count plastic canvas
- Worsted weight yarn as listed in color key
- #16 tapestry needle
- Black heavyweight thread

Christmas Seal
- 2 (⅜ inch/1cm) black shank buttons
- 16 (8mm) red sequins
- 16 red seed beads
- Red sewing thread
- 24 inches/61cm (⅛-inch/0.3cm-wide) red satin ribbon

Otter
- 2 (⅜ inch/1cm) black shank buttons
- 2 (8mm) red sequins
- 2 red seed beads
- Red sewing thread
- 30 inches/76.2cm (⅛-inch/0.3cm-wide) red satin ribbon

Walrus
- 2 (¼ inch/0.6cm) flat black buttons
- 14-inch/35.6cm strand miniature Christmas lights
- Sewing thread to match strand Christmas lights
- 12 inches/30.5cm (⅛-inch/0.3cm-wide) red satin ribbon

Cutting & Stitching

1. Cut plastic canvas according to graphs.

2. Stitch pieces following graphs, reversing one seal and one otter before stitching and working uncoded areas on pieces as follows: seal with white Continental Stitches, otter with tan Continental Stitches and walrus with light gray Continental Stitches.

Assembly

1. For water babies, using black heavyweight thread, attach eyes where indicated on graphs. For whiskers, thread 4-inch (10.2cm) lengths black heavyweight thread from back to front and tie over bars indicated; trim as desired.

2. Whipstitch wrong sides of water babies together.

3. For wreath, using red sewing thread, attach sequins with a bead on top where indicated. Whipstitch wrong

sides together along inside and outside edges. Tie a 6-inch (15.2cm) length red ribbon in a bow and glue to bottom of wreath front where indicated.

4. Whipstitch wrong sides of gift pieces together. Wrap a short length of red ribbon horizontally around center of gift, overlapping ends at center back; sew in place. Wrap a 12-inch (30.5cm) length of ribbon vertically around center of gift, tying together in a bow on top edge.

5. Using red sewing thread, attach sequins with a bead on top to both sides of gift where indicated.

6. Using photo as a guide, wrap Christmas lights strand around walrus; tack in place with matching thread.

7. For hangers, thread red ribbon through holes indicated on water babies. Tie ends together in a knot to form loops for hanging.

8. Place wreath over seal's head. Glue gift to otter's belly. ✂

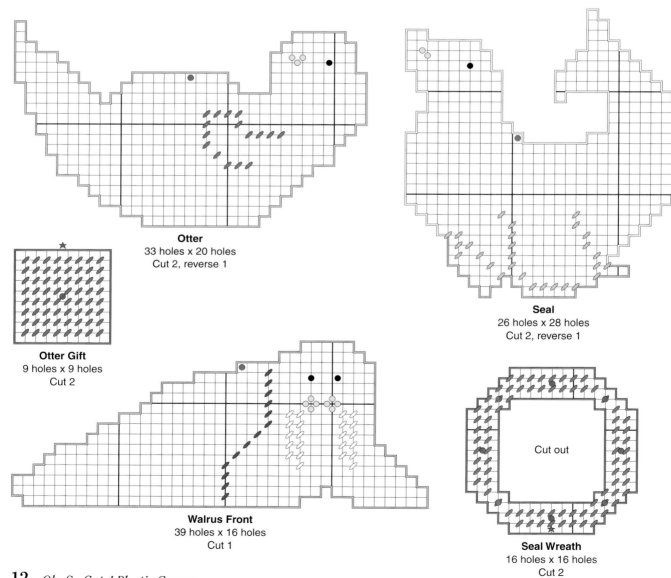

Otter
33 holes x 20 holes
Cut 2, reverse 1

Otter Gift
9 holes x 9 holes
Cut 2

Walrus Front
39 holes x 16 holes
Cut 1

Seal
26 holes x 28 holes
Cut 2, reverse 1

Seal Wreath
16 holes x 16 holes
Cut 2

Cut out

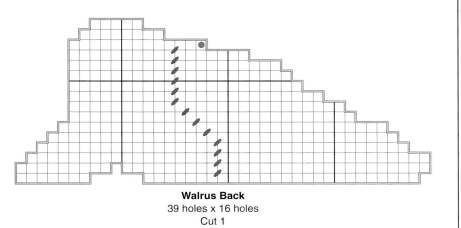

Walrus Back
39 holes x 16 holes
Cut 1

COLOR KEY	
Yards	**Worsted Weight Yarn**
18 (16.5m)	Light gray
17 (15.6m)	White
8 (7.4m)	Green
1 (1m)	Brown
1 (1m)	Dark gray
15 (13.8m)	Uncoded areas on otter are tan Continental Stitches
	Uncoded areas on seal are white Continental Stitches
	Uncoded areas on walrus are light gray Continental Stitches
	⁄ Tan Whipstitching
	● Attach button
	○ Attach whiskers
	● Attach sequin and seed bead
	★ Attach red ribbon bow
	● Attach hanging ribbon

Joy

Continued from page 10

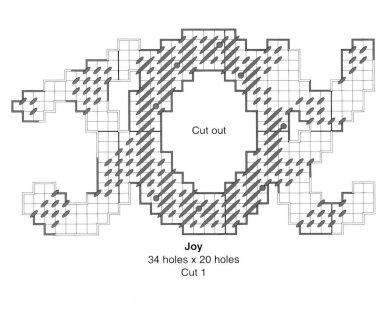

Cut out

Joy
34 holes x 20 holes
Cut 1

COLOR KEY	
Yards	**Worsted Weight Yarn**
4 (3.7m)	Dark green
3 (2.8m)	Gray
3 (2.8m)	Red
3 (2.8m)	Denim blue
1 (1m)	Pink
1 (1m)	Black
4 (3.7m)	Uncoded areas are white Continental Stitches
	⁄ White Overcasting
	⁄ Black Straight Stitch
	● Red (2-ply) French Knot
#5 Pearl Cotton	
1 (1m)	⁄ Black Backstitch and Straight Stitch
6-Strand Metallic Embroidery Floss	
1 (1m)	⁄ Gold #5282 (12-ply) Backstitch
Color number given is for DMC 6-strand metallic embroidery floss.	

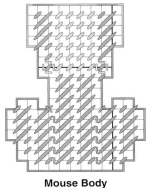

Mouse Body
13 holes x 16 holes
Cut 1

Festive Snowman Ornament

Choose your favorite winter-themed embellishments to accent and personalize this wintry friend.

Design by Laura Victory

Skill Level
Intermediate

Size
5 inches W x 4⅜ inches H x 4¾ inches D (12.7cm x 11.1cm x 12.1cm), excluding hanger

Materials
- 3-inch Uniek QuickShape plastic canvas 3-D globe
- 2 (3-inch) plastic canvas radial circles
- Uniek Needloft plastic canvas yarn as listed in color key
- Uniek Needloft solid metallic craft cord as listed in color key
- #16 tapestry needle
- 6 inches/15.2cm (⅜-inch/1cm-wide) gold ribbon
- 2 (18mm) movable eyes
- 3 (6mm) round black cabochons
- 1½-inch/3.8cm-long artificial carrot
- 2 (1-inch/25mm) green glitter pompoms
- Glitter or tinsel chenille stem in color of choice (sample used gold and white)
- Artificial sugared red berry spray with leaves
- Gold metallic thread
- Hot-glue gun

Instructions

1. Cut hat brim and hat top from 3-inch plastic canvas radial circles according to graphs, cutting away gray areas on radial circles (page 17). Cut one 27-hole x 8-hole piece for hat crown.

2. Stitch hat crown with black craft cord Continental Stitches. Stitch globe pieces (page 17), hat top and hat brim following graphs.

3. Using black craft cord, Whipstitch short edges of hat crown together, forming a circle, then Whipstitch top edge to hat top and bottom edge to hat brim. Overcast around outer edge of brim.

4. Connect head pieces. Place top piece in front and bottom piece in back. Cut chenille stem to fit around top half of head over seam; glue in place. Glue white yarn over bottom half along seam.

5. Use photo as a guide through step **7.** For earmuffs, glue green pompoms to head where chenille stem and yarn meet.

6. Glue carrot to center front for nose. Glue eyes in place on both sides of nose. Glue black cabochons below nose for mouth.

7. Wrap and glue gold ribbon around bottom of hat crown, allowing tails to hang over edge of brim. Cut apart red berry spray as desired and glue pieces to hat. Glue hat to top of head at a slight angle.

8. For hanger, cut desired length of gold thread. Thread through holes at top of hat; tie ends together in a knot to form a loop for hanging. ✂

Graphs continued on page 17

Beaded Stocking

Fill this checkered stocking with candy canes or other treats and keep snacks close at hand on your Christmas mantel. Design by Terry Ricioli

Skill Level
Beginner

Size
5¼ inches W x 8⅛ inches H (13.3cm x 20.6cm), excluding hanger

Materials
- 1 sheet 7-count plastic canvas
- Uniek Needloft plastic canvas yarn as listed in color key
- Kreinik ⅛-inch Ribbon as listed in color key
- #16 tapestry needle
- Black heavyweight thread
- 30 to 40 small red beads in various shapes and sizes

Instructions
1. Cut plastic canvas according to graph (page 20).

2. Stitch one stocking as graphed. Reverse second stocking and work stitches in reverse direction.

3. Using Christmas red throughout, Overcast top edges of stocking pieces. Whipstitch wrongs sides together along remaining edges.

4. Using photo as a guide, for fringe, attach various lengths of ribbon from back to front through adjacent holes where indicated, allowing tails to hang on the outside. Thread one to two beads on each tail and knot ribbon end.

5. For hanger, thread desired length of ribbon through top back holes of stocking where indicated with arrow. Tie ends together in a knot to form a loop for hanging. ✂

Graphs continued on page 20

Little Angel Hearts

Bring blessed beauty into your home with these sweet-faced angels. Carrying their glittering hearts on wings of love, you'll want to display them year-round.

Designs by Judy Collishaw

Skill Level
Beginner

Size
3 inches W x 4 inches H (7.6cm x 10.2cm), excluding hangers

Materials
- ¼ sheet 7-count plastic canvas
- 6 (3-inch) Darice plastic canvas heart shapes
- Worsted weight yarn as listed in color key
- Kreinik Heavy (#32) Braid as listed in color key
- #16 tapestry needle
- 6 (4mm) black beads
- 6 inches each ¼-inch/0.6cm-wide gold, silver and iridescent white ribbon
- 2 (6-inch/15.2cm) lengths thin silver cord
- 6 inches (15.2cm) thin gold cord
- Hand-sewing needle
- Black sewing thread
- Hot-glue gun

Instructions
1. Cut angel heads from plastic canvas according to graph.

2. Stitch and Overcast heads, working one as graphed, one replacing pale yellow with brown and one replacing pale yellow with rust.

3. Using hand-sewing needle and black thread, attach black beads for eyes where indicated on graph.

4. Stitch and Overcast wings, working one with coral rose as graphed, one with mint green and one with white.

5. Stitch angel robes following graphs. Do not Overcast. When background stitching is completed, work Star Cross Stitches, Smyrna Cross Stitches and French Knots.

6. Using photo as a guide, glue yellow-haired angel behind point of white robe, then glue coral rose wings behind head. In same manner, assemble brown-haired angel with pale blue robe and white wings, and rust-haired angel with yellow robe and mint wings.

7. Tie ends of thin gold cord together in a knot, forming a loop. Glue knot behind head of rust-haired angel. Repeat with silver cord, gluing behind heads of remaining angels.

8. Tie each ribbon in a bow. Glue gold bow to top of pale yellow robe, silver bow to top of white robe and iridescent white bow to top of pale blue robe. ✂

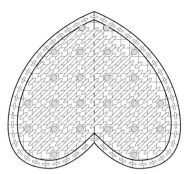

Yellow Robe
Stitch 1

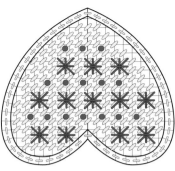

Blue Robe
Stitch 1

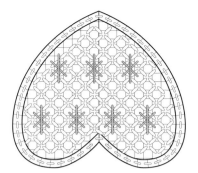

White Robe
Stitch 1

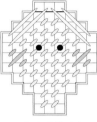

Angel Head
9 holes x 11 holes
Cut 3,
Stitch 1 as graphed
Stitch 1 replacing pale
yellow with brown
Stitch 1 replacing pale
yellow with rust

Angel Wings
Stitch 1 as graphed,
1 with mint green
and 1 with white

COLOR KEY

Yards	Worsted Weight Yarn
7 (6.5m)	□ White
5 (4.6m)	□ Pale yellow
5 (4.6m)	▨ Coral rose
4 (3.7m)	Mint green
4 (3.7m)	□ Pale blue
3 (2.8m)	□ Peach
1 (1m)	Rust
1 (1m)	Brown
	⁄ Coral rose Backstitch
	Heavy (#32) Braid
1 (1m)	✳ Silver hi lustre #001HL Star Cross Stitch
3 (2.8m)	✳ Pearl #032 Smyrna Cross Stitch
1 (1m)	○ Gold hi lustre French Knot
	● Pearl #032 French Knot
	● Attach black bead

Color numbers given are for Kreinik
Heavy (#32) Braid.

Festive Snowman Ornament

Continued from page 14

COLOR KEY

Yards	Plastic Canvas Yarn
18 (16.5m)	□ White #41
	Solid Metallic Craft Cord
5 (4.6m)	■ Solid black #55042

Color numbers given are for Uniek Needloft
plastic canvas yarn and solid metallic craft
cord.

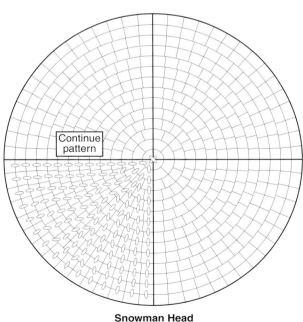

Continue
pattern

Snowman Head
Stitch top and bottom
halves of globe

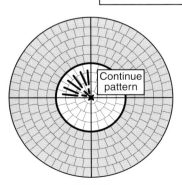

Continue
pattern

Hat Top
Cut 1 from radial circle,
cutting away gray area

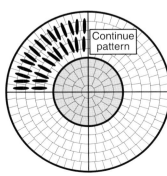

Continue
pattern

Hat Brim
Cut 1, cutting
away gray area

Holiday Tags

All the rage with paper crafters, tags are just as stylish when created in plastic canvas. Themed for the seasons, these tags are cute as gift embellishments or placed on display. Designs by Pam Bull

Skill Level
Beginner

Size
5¼ inches W x 2¾ inches H (13.3cm x 7cm), excluding ties

Materials
Each Tag
- 1 sheet 7-count plastic canvas
- Worsted weight yarn as listed in color key
- #16 tapestry needle
- Hot-glue gun

Pumpkin Patch Tag
- #3 pearl cotton as listed in color key
- 1 yard/1m 3-ply #28 jute twine
- ⅞-inch/2.2cm maroon star accent or button
- ⅞-inch/2.2cm round maroon button

Holiday Stocking Tag
- Coats & Clark Red Heart Holiday worsted weight yarn Art. N381 as listed in color key
- ½-inch/.5cm tan button

Country Charm Snowman
- #3 pearl cotton as listed in color key
- ½ x 1-inch (1.3cm x 2.5cm) cardboard triangle
- 2 (7mm) movable eyes
- ¾-inch/1.9cm maroon star button
- ¾-inch/1.9cm white snowflake accent or button

Instructions
1. Cut plastic canvas according to graphs (pages 19 and 20).

2. Stitch and Overcast pieces following graphs, working uncoded area on snowman with white yarn Continental Stitches. For snowman nose, wrap orange yarn evenly and tightly around cardboard triangle, gluing ends in place on back.

3. When background stitching and Overcasting are

completed, work lettering on tags with maroon yarn and black pearl cotton.

4. Use photo as a guide through step **9.** Tying yarn in front, attach buttons to pieces where indicated with blue dots as follows: maroon button to one pumpkin with maroon yarn; large star button to snowman hat brim with camel yarn; tan button to stocking cuff with maroon yarn.

5. Glue small star accent to remaining pumpkin or attach with maroon yarn if using button.

6. Glue pumpkin sides to backs of corresponding pumpkins, then glue assembled pumpkins to pumpkin tag. Glue stocking cuff to stocking, then glue to stocking

tag. Glue hat brim to snowman, then glue to snowman tag. Glue snowflake accent or button to snowman tag.

7. Attach remaining length of twine to pumpkin tag as in photo, trimming as needed.

8. For hangers, cut one each 18-inch/0.5m length of orange yarn and jute twine for pumpkin tag; white with silver and camel for stocking tag; heather blue and white for snowman tag.

9. Attach each pair of hangers to tags with a Lark's Head Knot, threading through hole in each tag. For stocking and snowman tags, tie ends of yarn together in a bow, making a loop for hanging; trim as desired. Tie orange yarn and jute twine in a bow next to tag; trim as desired. ✂

COLOR KEY

Yards	Worsted Weight Yarn
28 (25.7m)	☐ Tan
11 (10.1m)	☐ Orange
10 (9.2m)	☐ White with silver #3000
5 (4.6m)	▨ Maroon
4 (3.7m)	▨ Camel
3 (2.8m)	▨ Heather blue
3 (2.8m)	▨ Black
2 (1.9m)	▨ Green
3 (2.8m)	Uncoded area on snowman is white Continental Stitches
	⟋ White Overcasting
	⟋ Maroon Backstitch and Straight Stitch
	⟋ Green Backstitch and Straight Stitch
#3 Pearl Cotton	
4 (3.7m)	⟋ Black Backstitch and Straight Stitch
	● Attach button

Color number given is for Coats & Clark Red Heart Holiday worsted weight yarn Art. N381.

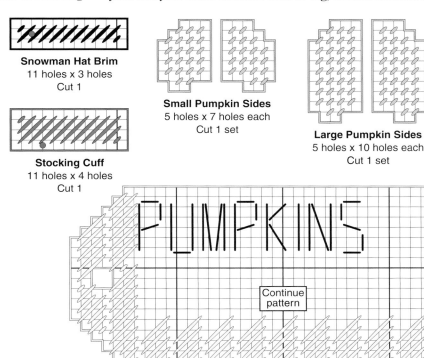

Snowman Hat Brim
11 holes x 3 holes
Cut 1

Stocking Cuff
11 holes x 4 holes
Cut 1

Small Pumpkin Sides
5 holes x 7 holes each
Cut 1 set

Large Pumpkin Sides
5 holes x 10 holes each
Cut 1 set

Pumpkin Patch Tag
34 holes x 18 holes
Cut 1

Continue pattern

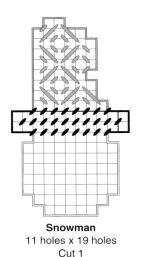

Snowman
11 holes x 19 holes
Cut 1

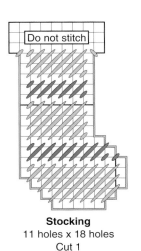

Stocking
11 holes x 18 holes
Cut 1

Do not stitch

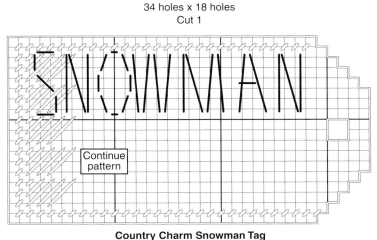

Continue pattern

Country Charm Snowman Tag
34 holes x 18 holes
Cut 1

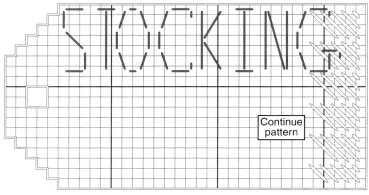

Holiday Stocking Tag
34 holes x 18 holes
Cut 1

Continue pattern

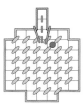

Small Pumpkin
7 holes x 9 holes
Cut 1

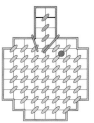

Large Pumpkin
8 holes x 11 holes
Cut 1

Beaded Stocking

Continued from page 15

Continued from page 15

COLOR KEY

Yards	Plastic Canvas Yarn
24 (22m)	■ Red #01
14 (15.6m)	□ White #41

1/8-Inch Ribbon

5 1/2 (5m)	● Attach white #100 fringe

Color numbers given are for Uniek Needloft plastic canvas yarn and Kreinik 1/8-inch Ribbon.

Beaded Stocking
38 holes x 57 holes
Cut 2
Stitch 1 as graphed
Reverse 1 and work
stitches in reverse direction

Noah's Ark Suncatcher

Add cheer to your day with this colorful suncatcher featuring just a few of Noah's animals. Beads and wire add a contemporary look.

Design by Mary T. Cosgrove

Skill Level
Beginner

Size
10 inches W x 11¼ inches H (25.4cm x 28.6cm)

Materials
- ⅔ sheet 7-count plastic canvas
- Uniek Needloft plastic canvas yarn as listed in color key
- #16 tapestry needle
- 7-inch/17.8cm gold craft ring
- 6 (7mm) movable eyes
- 5½ inches/12.7cm royal blue and gold beaded fringe
- 6 (12 x 10mm) royal blue heart beads
- Off-white felt
- 1 yard (1m) brown craft wire
- Needle-nose pliers
- Pencil
- Fabric glue

Cutting & Stitching
1. Cut plastic canvas according to graphs. Cut off-white felt to match each shape.

2. Stitch and Overcast pieces following graphs, working uncoded areas on ark and lion with beige Continental Stitches, uncoded area on dove with white Continental Stitches and uncoded area on elephant with gray Continental Stitches.

3. When background stitching is completed, work maple embroidery on lion and cinnamon embroidery on ark and dove.

Assembly
1. Use photo as a guide throughout assembly. Glue movable eyes to lion, giraffe and elephant where indicated.

2. Cut desired length of yarn for tails as follows: maple for lion, yellow for giraffe and gray for elephant. Tie a knot in each length about ½ inch (1.3cm) from one end. Attach remaining ends to backs of pieces where indicated with black arrows.

3. Using matching yarn throughout, tack back of rainbow to top right of gold craft ring. Tack back of dove to top left of ring. Tack top of ark to bottom left of rainbow.

4. Cut four 3-inch/7.6cm lengths of brown craft wire. Use two lengths to secure ark where indicated to side of gold ring. Wrap remaining two lengths around pencil, then attach one each to backs of dove and rainbow along bottom edges at green arrows.

5. Thread one heart bead on bottom of each of these lengths; bring wire up at back of bead; twist to wire at top of bead to secure.

6. Glue bead fringe along bottom edge of ark, trimming as needed to fit.

7. Cut four 6-inch/15.2cm lengths brown craft wire. Attach one length each to lion, giraffe and elephant where indicated. Twist wire and add one heart bead to each length, then wire to bottom and sides (at same place ark is secured) of craft ring.

8. Use last length of wire for hanger, adding heart bead and making a loop for hanging.

9. Glue felt to backs of pieces, trimming as needed to fit. *Note: For dove and rainbow, felt will need to be glued over ring.* ✄

Graphs continued on page 25

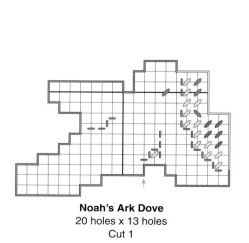

Noah's Ark Dove
20 holes x 13 holes
Cut 1

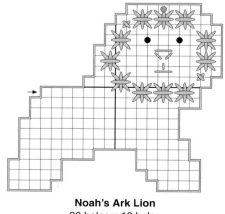

Noah's Ark Lion
20 holes x 18 holes
Cut 1

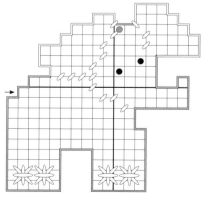

Noah's Ark Elephant
18 holes x 18 holes
Cut 1

Baby Buggy

Celebrate the arrival of a new baby with a miniature buggy sized just right for a package of hard candies or gum. Design by Deborah Scheblein

Skill Level
Beginner

Size
3 inches W x 3¼ inches H x 1⅜ inches D
(7.6cm x 8.3cm x 3.5cm)

Materials
- ¼ sheet 7-count plastic canvas
- 2 (3-inch) plastic canvas radial circles
- Worsted weight yarn as listed in color key
- #16 tapestry needle
- 6 inches/15.2cm (⅛-inch/0.3cm-wide) pink or blue satin ribbon
- Hot-glue gun

Instructions
1. Cut plastic canvas according to graphs, cutting away gray areas on plastic canvas radial circles for wheels.

2. Following graphs throughout, stitch and Overcast wheels. Stitch carriage and base pieces, reversing one carriage piece before stitching.

3. Whipstitch wrongs sides of carriage pieces together around top and sides from blue dot to blue dot. Spread apart bottom half of carriage, then Whipstitch base to bottom edges. Overcast all remaining edges.

4. Using photo as a guide, glue wheels to bottom portion of carriage front. Tie ribbon in a bow and glue to carriage front where indicated on graph. ✄

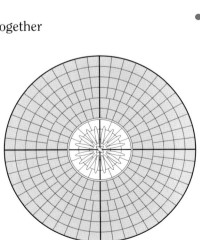

Baby Carriage
19 holes x 21 holes
Cut 2, reverse 1

Baby Carriage Base
11 holes x 7 holes
Cut 1

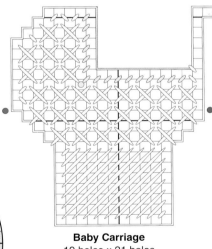

Baby Carriage Wheel
Cut 2 from plastic canvas radial circles, cutting away gray areas

COLOR KEY	
Yards	**Worsted Weight Yarn**
4 (3.7m)	☐ White
1 (1m)	☐ Pink or blue
	○ Attach ribbon bow

Patriotic Angel

Cute as can be, this little angel is letting her patriotic pride soar. This project can also be finished as a magnet. Design by Debbie Tabor

Materials

- ¼ sheet 7-count plastic canvas
- Coats & Clark Red Heart Classic worsted weight yarn Art. E267 as listed in color key
- Coats & Clark Red Heart Super Saver worsted weight yarn Art. E300 as listed in color key
- 6-strand embroidery floss as listed in color key
- #16 tapestry needle

Instructions

1. Cut plastic canvas according to graph.

2. Stitch piece following graph, working uncoded areas with sea coral Continental Stitches. Do not Overcast edges.

3. Work gold Loop Stitches (see diagram) where indicated. Using 3 plies floss, work remaining embroidery, passing over eyes three times and wrapping white French Knots three times.

4. Hang as desired. ✂

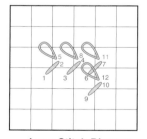

Loop Stitch Diagram
Bring needle up at 1, down at 2, up at 3, down at 4.
Bring needle up and down at 5, making a loop.
Bring needle back up at 6, being careful not to pull loop back down through hole.
Continue pattern until Loop Stitches are completed, making 1 last Loop Stitch (see No. 12).

Skill Level
Beginner

Size
4¼ inches W x 5 inches H (10.8cm x 12.7cm), excluding hanger

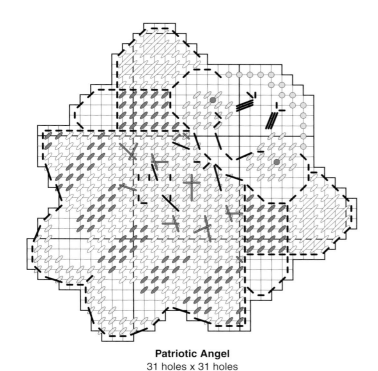

Patriotic Angel
31 holes x 31 holes
Cut 1

COLOR KEY

Yards	Worsted Weight Yarn
2 (1.9m)	☐ White #311
1 (1m)	☐ Rose pink #372
3 (2.8m)	■ Hot red #390
1 (1m)	☐ Mist green #681
3 (2.8m)	☐ Delft blue #885
3 (2.8m)	Uncoded areas are sea coral #246 Continental Stitches
2 (1.9m)	◎ Gold #321 Loop Stitch
	6-Strand Embroidery Floss
1 (1m)	╱ Black (3-ply) Backstitch and Straight Stitch
1 (1m)	╱ White (3-ply) Backstitch and Straight Stitch
	● White (3-ply/3-wrap) French Knot

Color numbers given are for Coats & Clark Red Heart Classic worsted weight yarn Art. E267 and Super Saver worsted weight yarn Art. E300.

Noah's Ark Suncatcher

Continued from page 22

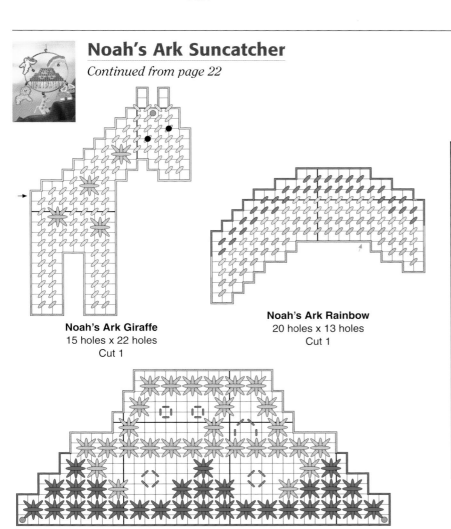

Noah's Ark Giraffe
15 holes x 22 holes
Cut 1

Noah's Ark Rainbow
20 holes x 13 holes
Cut 1

COLOR KEY

Yards	Plastic Canvas Yarn
2 (1.9m)	■ Christmas red #02
6 (5.5m)	☐ Maple #13
3 (2.8m)	■ Cinnamon #14
1 (1m)	■ Holly #27
4 (3.7m)	■ Royal #32
4 (3.7m)	☐ Beige #40
4 (3.7m)	☐ White #41
5 (4.6m)	☐ Yellow #57
3 (2.8m)	■ Bright orange #58
1 (1m)	☐ Bright blue #60
	Uncoded areas on ark and lion are beige #40 Continental Stitches
	Uncoded area on dove is white #41 Continental Stitches
3 (2.8m)	Uncoded area on elephant is gray #38 Continental Stitches
	╱ Maple #13 Backstitch and Straight Stitch
	╱ Cinnamon #14 Backstitch
	╱ Gray #38 Overcasting
	● Attach movable eye
	◎ Attach brown craft wire

Color numbers given are for Uniek Needloft plastic canvas yarn.

Noah's Ark
35 holes x 15 holes
Cut 1

Cute Containers

Keep organized yet stylish with a variety of catch-alls. From a cell phone cozy to goodie boxes, you'll love stitching these designs.

Kitty Cell Cozy & Key Chain

Protect your cell phone with a cute kitten case. The coordinating key ring makes this a must-have for any cat lover. Designs by Lee Lindeman

Skill Level
Beginner

Size
Kitty Cell Cozy: 2⅜ inches W x 4¾ inches H x 1 inch D (6cm x 12.1cm x 2.5cm)

Mouse Key Chain: 2⅝ inches W x 1⅝ inches H (6.7cm x 4.2cm), excluding tail

Materials
- 1 sheet 7-count plastic canvas
- Uniek Needloft plastic canvas yarn as listed in color key
- 6-strand embroidery floss as listed in color key
- #16 tapestry needle
- Small amount pink craft foam
- Small amount gray faux suede or felt
- 2 (9mm) blue cat eyes
- 2 (4mm) black beads
- 3 (⁵⁄₁₆-inch/0.8cm) red heart buttons
- Small amount polyester fiberfill
- Wire cutters or sharp craft scissors (optional)
- Hot-glue gun

Cutting & Stitching
1. Cut plastic canvas according to graphs. Cut one 6-hole x 60-hole piece for gusset and one 5-hole by 6-hole piece for hinge.

2. Cut one nose from pink craft foam and two ears from gray faux suede or felt using patterns given. For tail, depending on number of keys, cut desired length of one ³⁄₁₆-inch/0.5cm-wide piece of gray faux suede or felt, cutting one end to a point. Set aside.

3. Work gusset and hinge with black Continental Stitches. Stitch remaining pieces following graphs, reversing one mouse before stitching and working uncoded areas on kitty face and front with black Continental Stitches.

4. For whiskers, place a 1-inch (4.4cm) length of white yarn on face where indicated, then work Backstitches with 2 plies black floss, working vertical stitch tightly over whiskers. Fray ends of whiskers.

Kitty Cell Cozy Assembly

1. Using black throughout, Whipstitch long edges of gusset around side and bottom edges of front and back from arrow to arrow, easing as necessary to fit. Whipstitch 5-hole edges of hinge to back and face where indicated on graphs. Overcast all remaining cozy edges.

2. If red heart buttons have shanks, cut off shanks with wire cutters or sharp craft scissors. Glue buttons to front where indicated on graph.

3. Glue nose and eyes to face.

Mouse Key Chain Assembly

1. Using black floss, sew beads to mouse.

2. Place a small amount of fiberfill between mouse pieces, then Whipstitch together with colors indicated, inserting straight end of tail between layers at arrow while Whipstitching. Before closing, glue tail on inside to secure.

3. Fold pointed end of ears together and glue, then glue pointed ends to mouse where indicated.

4. Thread keys on end of tail, fold tip over and glue to tail. ✄

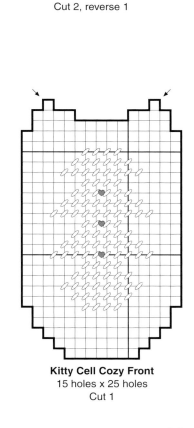

Key Chain Mouse
17 holes x 10 holes
Cut 2, reverse 1

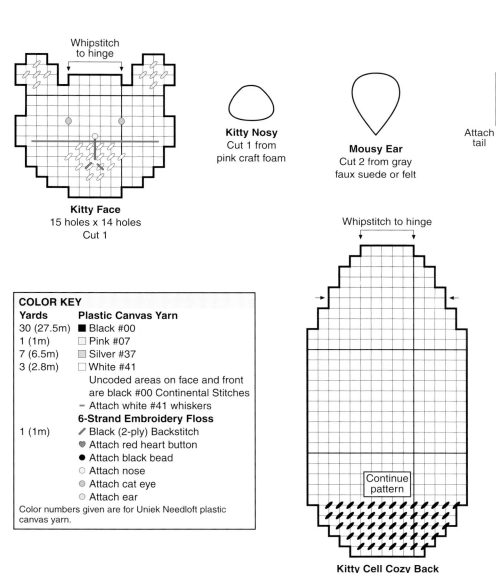

Kitty Face
15 holes x 14 holes
Cut 1

Kitty Nosy
Cut 1 from
pink craft foam

Mousy Ear
Cut 2 from gray
faux suede or felt

COLOR KEY

Yards	Plastic Canvas Yarn
30 (27.5m)	■ Black #00
1 (1m)	□ Pink #07
7 (6.5m)	▨ Silver #37
3 (2.8m)	□ White #41
	Uncoded areas on face and front are black #00 Continental Stitches
	– Attach white #41 whiskers
	6-Strand Embroidery Floss
1 (1m)	✎ Black (2-ply) Backstitch
	♥ Attach red heart button
	● Attach black bead
	○ Attach nose
	◉ Attach cat eye
	○ Attach ear

Color numbers given are for Uniek Needloft plastic canvas yarn.

Kitty Cell Cozy Back
15 holes x 30 holes
Cut 1

Kitty Cell Cozy Front
15 holes x 25 holes
Cut 1

Mini Butterfly Tote

Imagine the look of surprise on your little girl's face when you give her a butterfly purse of her very own! Design by Kathy Wirth

Skill Level
Intermediate

Size
3¾ inches W x 5⅞ inches H x 2 inches D (9.5cm x 15cm x 5.1cm), excluding antennae

Materials
- ½ sheet 7-count plastic canvas
- 2 (6-inch) Uniek QuickShape plastic canvas hearts
- Uniek Needloft plastic canvas yarn as listed in color key
- #16 tapestry needle
- 1 yard (1m) 26-gauge black wire
- 4 black E beads
- ⅛-inch/0.3cm dowel or large nail
- Wire cutters
- Needle-nose pliers

Instructions

1. Cut plastic canvas according to graphs (page 55), cutting away gray areas on front and back. Cut one 16-hole x 12-hole pieces for tote bottom. Tote bottom will remain unstitched.

2. Stitch pieces following graphs working uncoded areas with bright purple Continental Stitches.

3. Using bright purple through step 4, Overcast inside edges of handles, outside edges of handles from purple dot to purple dot and top edges of sides.

4. Whipstitch front, back and sides to bottom. Beginning at bottom and easing around curves to fit, Whipstitch sides to front and back, working up to handles on front and back.

5. For antennae, cut wire in two 18-inch/0.5m lengths. Thread ends of one wire from back to front through holes indicated on front. Pull wire clear through making ends even on outside. To secure, twist wires together close to stitching.

6. Thread one E bead onto each wire end, then run wire ends back through bead; tighten to secure. Trim wire end flush with bead.

7. Wrap each wire antenna tightly around dowel or nail, pushing coils together. Remove dowel; arrange antennae as in photo.

8. Repeat with remaining wire on tote back. ✄

Graphs continued on page 55

Gone Fishin' Card Holder

Delight in the chuckle you'll get from your favorite fisherman when you give him this whimsical card holder. Design by Ronda Bryce

Skill Level
Intermediate

Size
4⅞ inches W x 2½ inches H x 4 inches D (12.4cm x 6.4cm x 10.2cm), including sign and creel

Materials
- ½ sheet 7-count plastic canvas
- 2 (3-inch) Uniek QuickShape plastic canvas radial circles
- Uniek Needloft plastic canvas yarn as listed in color key
- Lion Brand Wool-Ease worsted weight yarn Article #620 as listed in color key
- Coats & Clark Red Heart Classic worsted weight yarn Art. E267 as listed in color key
- 6-strand embroidery floss as listed in color key
- #16 tapestry needle
- 8½ inches/21.6cm (⅛-inch/0.3cm-wide) medium brown leather suede lace
- 6mm round dark brown wood bead
- 2 (1-inch/2.5cm) fish buttons
- Red party toothpick
- Hand-sewing needle
- Beige sewing thread

Cutting
1. Cut plastic canvas according to graphs (page 32), cutting away gray areas on creel lid and bottom.

2. Cut 100 (7-inch/17.8cm) lengths paddy green yarn. Set aside.

3. Cut leather suede lace so there is one 2½-inch/6.4cm length and one 6-inch/15.2cm length. Set aside.

Base
1. Stitch and Overcast base with royal where indicated on graph.

2. Using 100 lengths paddy green yarn, work Lark's Head Knots where indicated. Trim to about ½-inch/1.3cm long. Overcast adjacent edges with paddy green.

3. Using hand-sewing needle and beige sewing thread, sew one fish button to base where indicated on graph.

Holder
1. Stitch holder pieces following graphs. Overcast top edges.

2. Whipstitch front and back to sides, then Whipstitch front, back and sides to unstitched area on base, Whipstitching bottom edge of front to purple highlighted line on base.

Creel

1. Stitch creel pieces following graphs, leaving creel bottom unstitched.

2. Using camel throughout, Overcast top edge of front. Whipstitch side edges of creel front to side edges of creel back, then Whipstitch unstitched base to front and back.

3. Using cinnamon, Overcast round edge of lid from yellow dot to yellow dot, then Whipstitch remaining edge to top edge of back.

4. Use hand-sewing needle and beige sewing thread through step 7. For handle, tack ends of 6-inch/15.2cm length of leather suede lace to both sides of creel front where indicated on graph.

5. With tail inside, sew fish to top edge of creel front where indicated.

6. For closure, tack ends of 2½-inch/6.4cm-length

leather suede lace to wrong side of lid where indicated on graph, forming a loop. Sew bead to creel front where indicated. Put loop over bead

7. Tack back of creel to right side of holder front.

Sign

1. Stitch and Overcast sign pieces following graphs, working uncoded backgrounds with sandstone Continental Stitches. Embroider lettering with floss when background stitching and Overcasting are completed.

2. With "GONE" sign on top, Whipstitch signs together along edges, using hand-sewing needle and beige thread. Insert red toothpick through stitches on back of sign.

3. Insert toothpick into "grass" in front of holder (see photo). Using hand-sewing needle and beige thread, tack back of sign to holder front. ✂

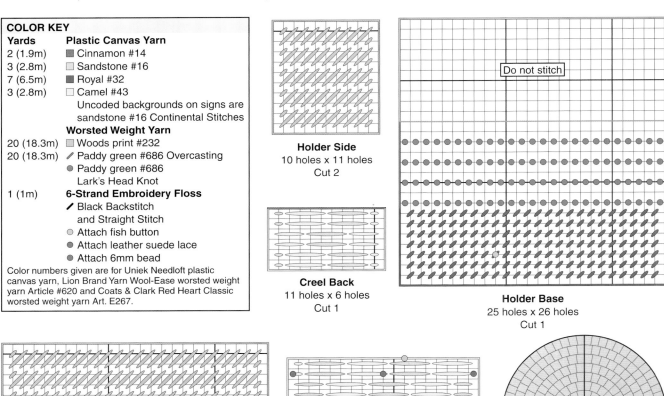

COLOR KEY

Yards	Plastic Canvas Yarn
2 (1.9m)	■ Cinnamon #14
3 (2.8m)	□ Sandstone #16
7 (6.5m)	■ Royal #32
3 (2.8m)	□ Camel #43
	Uncoded backgrounds on signs are sandstone #16 Continental Stitches

	Worsted Weight Yarn
20 (18.3m)	□ Woods print #232
20 (18.3m)	╱ Paddy green #686 Overcasting
	● Paddy green #686 Lark's Head Knot

	6-Strand Embroidery Floss
1 (1m)	╱ Black Backstitch and Straight Stitch
	○ Attach fish button
	● Attach leather suede lace
	● Attach 6mm bead

Color numbers given are for Uniek Needloft plastic canvas yarn, Lion Brand Yarn Wool-Ease worsted weight yarn Article #620 and Coats & Clark Red Heart Classic worsted weight yarn Art. E267.

Holder Side
10 holes x 11 holes
Cut 2

Creel Back
11 holes x 6 holes
Cut 1

Holder Base
25 holes x 26 holes
Cut 1

Holder Front & Back
25 holes x 11 holes
Cut 2

Creel Front
18 holes x 6 holes
Cut 1

Creel Lid & Bottom
Cut 2 from 3-inch
plastic canvas radial circles,
cutting away gray area
Stitch lid only

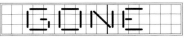

Gone Sign
17 holes x 3 holes
Cut 1

Fishin' Sign
17 holes x 3 holes
Cut 1

Cool School Tools

Add some fun to your work area with this trendy floral desk set.
Bright colors add to the charm of this useful set. Designs by Debra Arch

Skill Level
Beginner

Size
Pencil Port: 4½ inches H x 4 inches in diameter (11.4cm x 10.2cm)

Paper Port: 3½ inches W x 3 inches H x 3½ inches D (8.9cm x 7.6cm x 8.9cm) Fits 2⅞-inch square (73mm) paper notes

Postage Port: 1⅛ inches H x 2⅞ inches in diameter (2.9cm x 7.3cm)

Materials
- 2 sheets clear stiff 7-count plastic canvas
- 2 sheets bright pink 7-count plastic canvas
- 3 (4-inch) Uniek QuickShape plastic canvas radial circles
- Uniek Needloft plastic canvas yarn as listed in color key
- #16 tapestry needle
- Hot-glue gun

Pencil Port

1. Cut one pencil port side from clear stiff plastic canvas according to graph (page 35). Cut one 73-hole x 28-hole piece from bright pink plastic canvas for lining. Cut the outermost row of holes from one 4-inch plastic canvas radial circle for base. Lining and base will remain unstitched.

2. Stitch side following graph, working uncoded background with tangerine Continental Stitches.

3. When background stitching is completed, work Lazy Daisy Stitches for flowers as graphed. Work French Knots for flower centers with a double strand yarn.

4. Using tangerine throughout, Whipstitch side edges of side together, forming a cylinder. Overcast top edge; Whipstitch bottom edge to unstitched base.

5. Using bright pink yarn, Whipstitch side edges of lining together, forming center back seam. Overcast top edge.

6. Place lining inside pencil port, aligning seams. Using bright pink, Whipstitch top edges together with a Blanket Stitch.

Paper Port

1. Cut one paper port front and three side/back pieces from clear stiff plastic canvas; cut one front and three side/back pieces from bright pink plastic canvas for lining according to graphs. Also cut two 22-hole x 22-hole pieces from pink for base. Lining and base pieces will remain unstitched.

2. Stitch clear stiff pieces following graphs, working uncoded backgrounds with tangerine Continental Stitches.

3. Using tangerine throughout, align one lining piece behind front, back and side pieces, then Whipstitch front and back to sides through all thicknesses. Overcast top edges. Place base pieces together and Whipstitch to front, back and sides.

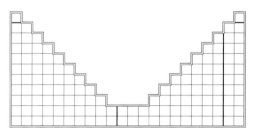

Paper Port Front
22 holes x 11 holes
Cut 1 from clear stiff
Stitch with tangerine Continental Stitches
Cut 1 from bright pink for lining
Do not stitch

Postage Port

1. Cut one flower and one lid side from clear stiff plastic canvas according to graphs. Also cut one 52-hole x 4-hole piece for box side from clear stiff. Box side will remain unstitched.

2. Cut lid top from one 4-inch plastic canvas radial circle following graph, cutting away gray areas. Cut the six outermost rows of holes from remaining 4-inch plastic canvas radial circle for box base. Base will remain unstitched.

3. Following graphs throughout, stitch and Overcast flower following graph. Stitch lid top, following pattern around circle.

4. Using tangerine through step 5, Whipstitch side edges of lid side together, forming a circle, then Whipstitch lid side to lid top. Overcast bottom edges of side. Inside edges of lid top will remain unstitched.

5. Whipstitch side edges of unstitched box side together, forming a circle, then Whipstitch to unstitched base. Overcast top edges of box side.

6. Center flower on lid top and tack in place with bright pink yarn. Insert roll of stamps in box. Thread first stamp through opening in lid; place lid on box. ✂

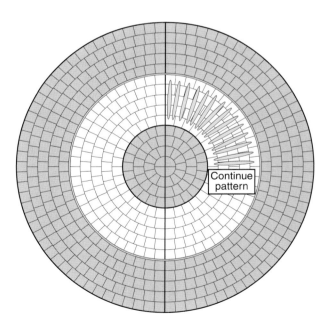

Postage Port Lid Top
Cut 1 from 4-inch plastic
canvas radial circle,
cutting away gray areas

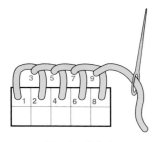

Blanket Stitch
Bring needle up at 1, form a loop and bring needle down at 2. Bring needle up through loop at 3, over yarn and down at 4, etc.

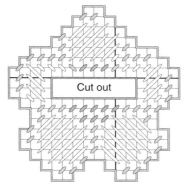

Postage Port Flower
16 holes x 17 holes
Cut 1 from clear stiff

COLOR KEY

Yards	Plastic Canvas Yarn
80 (73.2m)	☐ Tangerine #11
14 (12.9m)	☐ White #41
11 (10.1m)	▨ Bright orange #58
19 (17.4m)	▨ Bright pink #62
	Uncoded backgrounds are tangerine #11 Continental Stitches
	⟐ White #41 Lazy Daisy Stitch
	⟐ Bright orange #58 Lazy Daisy Stitch
	⟐ Bright pink #62 Lazy Daisy Stitch
	○ White #41 (2-strand) French Knot
	● Bright orange #58 (2-strand) French Knot
	○ Bright pink #62 (2-strand) French Knot

Color numbers given are for Uniek Needloft plastic canvas yarn.

Continue pattern

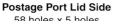

Postage Port Lid Side
58 holes x 5 holes
Cut 1 from clear stiff

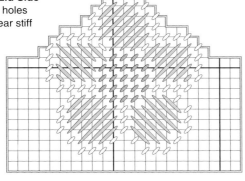

Paper Port Side/Back
22 holes x 18 holes
Cut 3 from clear stiff
Stitch as graphed
Cut 3 from bright pink for lining
Do not stitch

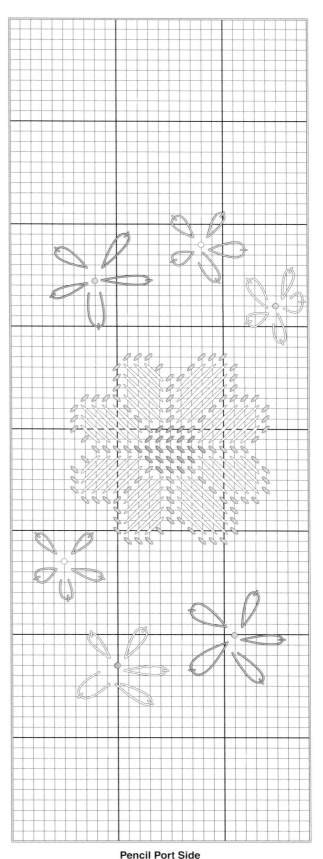

Pencil Port Side
80 holes x 28 holes
Cut 1 from clear stiff

Halloween Surprise

These adorable Halloween critters aren't scaring a soul this year; they're just too cute! Fill this tote with candy and use as a delightful centerpiece. Design by Janelle Giese

Skill Level
Intermediate

Size
5½ inches W x 6 inches H x 2⅞ inches D
(14 cm x 15.2cm x 7.3cm)

Materials
- ½ sheet clear 7-count plastic canvas
- ¾ sheet bright purple 7-count plastic canvas
- Uniek Needloft plastic canvas yarn as listed in color key
- #5 pearl cotton as listed in color key
- DMC 6-strand embroidery floss as listed in color key
- #16 tapestry needle

Project Note
The diamond, heart, star, square, triangle and inverted triangle shapes designate Continental Stitches.

Instructions
1. Cut one front from clear plastic canvas according to graph. From bright purple plastic canvas, cut one 26-hole x 33-hole piece for back, two 18-hole x 33-hole pieces for sides and one 26-hole x 18-hole piece for base. Back, sides and base will remain unstitched.

2. Stitch front following graph, working uncoded background with black yarn Continental Stitches and leaving blue highlighted lines (Whipstitch lines) unworked at this time.

3. On front, Overcast top edges around hands, arms and head from arrow to arrow and extended side edges from arrow to arrow.

4. When background stitching is completed, work Cross Stitches for cheeks with 2-plies salmon.

5. Straight Stitch fangs with white yarn and eyes of vampire and ghost with black yarn. Split a strand of white yarn and work Pin Stitch in each eye as follows: Bring yarn up in hole indicated above stitch, go down through black yarn, splitting stitch and going back down through same hole in which stitch originated.

6. Work pearl cotton embroidery, forming Straight Stitches on sides of each fang and eyes of vampire and eyes on ghost. Work French Knots for eyes of witch, wrapping pearl cotton two times.

7. Work bright orange Straight Stitches for witch's hair.

8. Using black yarn, Whipstitch sides to back. Whipstitch sides to front following graph, working Continental Stitches in colors indicated on blue highlighted lines. Whipstitch base to back and sides with black and to front with colors indicated on front graph. ✄

COLOR KEY

Yards	Plastic Canvas Yarn
1 (1m)	⬦ Red #01
3 (2.8m)	◇ White #41
1 (1m)	⬭ Camel #43
1 (1m)	▼ Purple #46
3 (2.8m)	■ Bittersweet #52
2 (1.9m)	♡ Pale peach #56
1 (1m)	☆ Yellow #57
3 (2.8m)	◆ Bright orange #58
4 (3.7m)	△ Bright green #61
2 (1.9m)	⬭ Bright purple #64
9 (8.3m)	Uncoded background is black #00 Continental Stitches
	⬭ Black #00 Straight Stitch, Overcasting and Whipstitching
	⬭ White #41 (2-ply) Straight Stitch
	⬭ White #41 (1-ply) Pin Stitch
	⬭ Bright orange #58 Straight Stitch
	#5 Pearl Cotton
8 (7.4m)	⬭ Black Backstitch and Straight Stitch
	● Black (2-wrap) French Knot
	6-Strand Embroidery Floss
1 (1m)	✕ Salmon #760 Cross Stitch

Color numbers given are for Uniek Needloft plastic canvas yarn and DMC 6-strand embroidery floss.

Halloween Surprise Tote Front
36 holes x 39 holes
Cut 1 from clear

North Pole Goodie Boxes

Fill these boxes with nuts or candy and delight Mr. and Mrs. Claus with a surprise treat. Designs by Judy Collishaw

Materials

- 1 sheet 7-count plastic canvas
- Worsted weight yarn as listed in color key
- #5 pearl cotton as listed in color key
- #16 tapestry needle
- ¼-inch/7mm white pompom
- 2 (4mm) black beads
- 9 inches/22.9cm ⅛-inch/0.3cm-wide green satin ribbon
- Hand-sewing needle
- Black sewing thread
- Hot-glue gun

Skill Level
Beginner

Size
Santa Claus: 2¾ inches W x 5⅛ inches H x 2¼ inches D (7cm x 13cm x 5.7cm)
Mrs. Claus: 2¼ inches W x 5¼ inches H x 2¼ inches D (5.7cm x 13.3cm x 5.7cm)

Instructions

1. Cut plastic canvas according to graphs. Cut two 14-hole x 14-hole pieces for box bases.

2. Stitch and Overcast heads following graphs, working uncoded areas with pale peach Continental Stitches.

3. When background stitching and Overcasting on heads are completed, work the following yarn embroidery on Santa Claus' head: white Straight Stitches for eyebrows and mustache, red French Knot for nose, wrapping yarn three times and black Straight Stitches for eyes. Work red pearl cotton Backstitches for mouth.

4. On Mrs. Claus' head, work red pearl cotton Backstitches for mouth. Attach beads for eyes where indicated with hand-sewing needle and black sewing thread.

5. Stitch remaining pieces following graphs. When background stitching is completed, work black Straight Stitch on Santa Claus' belt buckle.

6. Overcast top edges of box fronts from arrow to arrow. Overcast top edges of backs and sides.

7. For each box, Whipstitch front, back and sides together, then Whipstitch front, back and sides to unstitched base.

8. Using photo as a guide, glue heads to top of corresponding box fronts. Glue pompom to tip of Santa Claus' hat. Tie green ribbon in a bow and glue under chin on Mrs. Claus. Tie a 6-inch length of white yarn in a bow and glue to box back where indicated on graph. ✂

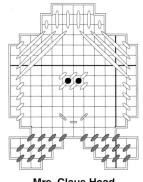

Mrs. Claus Head
12 holes x 16 holes
Cut 1

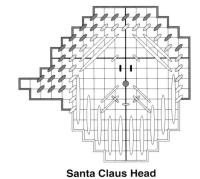

Santa Claus Head
16 holes x 15 holes
Cut 1

COLOR KEY	
Yards	**Worsted Weight Yarn**
20 (18.3m)	▨ Red
7 (6.5m)	☐ White
2 (1.9m)	■ Black
1 (1m)	▨ Burgundy
1 (1m)	☐ Yellow
1 (1m)	☐ Off-white
2 (1.9m)	Uncoded areas are pale peach Continental Stitches
	╱ Pale peach Overcasting
	╱ White Straight Stitch
	╱ Black Straight Stitch
	● Red (3-wrap) French Knot
	● Attach white yarn bow
	#3 Pearl Cotton
1 (1m)	╱ Red Backstitch
	● Attach black bead

Santa Claus Box Side/Back
14 holes x 14 holes
Cut 3

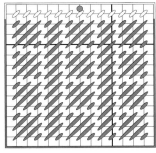

Mrs. Claus Box Side/Back
14 holes x 14 holes
Cut 3

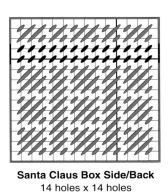

Mrs. Claus Box Front
14 holes x 24 holes
Cut 1

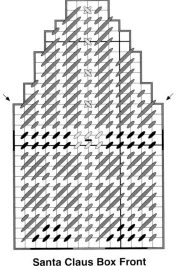

Santa Claus Box Front
14 holes x 24 holes
Cut 1

Regal Cardinal

Use this cheerful cardinal container to store handfuls of candy or a small potted plant. Design by Debra Arch

Skill Level
Advanced

Size
9⅜ inches W x 7¾ inches H x 4¼ inches D
(23.8cm x 19.7cm x 10.8cm), including wings

Materials
- 3 sheets clear 7-count plastic canvas
- 1 sheet red 7-count plastic canvas
- Uniek Needloft plastic canvas yarn as listed in color key
- #16 tapestry needle
- 2 (10mm) white pearl shank buttons
- Wire cutters
- Hot-glue gun

Cutting & Stitching

1. Cut two body pieces, two wings, one breast, one tail top, one tail back and one beak base from clear plastic canvas according to graphs (this page and pages 42 and 48).

2. Cut one lining front, two lining sides and one lining back from red plastic canvas according to graphs (this page and pages 42 and 48). From red plastic canvas, also cut one 27-hole x 21-hole piece for cardinal base. Lining pieces and base will remain unstitched.

3. Following graphs throughout stitching and assembly, stitch beak base, breast and body pieces, reversing one body piece before stitching and using a double strand when stitching with red yarn.

4. Stitch tail top and tail back with a Close Herringbone Stitch (page 42), using 1 strand red yarn.

5. Stitch and Overcast wings, reversing one before stitching. Work Close Herringbone Stitches first, using 1 strand and finishing rows as shown on wing graph, then work Slanted Gobelin Stitches with a double strand, working some stitches over Close Herringbone Stitches as indicated.

Assembly

1. Whipstitch wrong sides of body pieces together along head edges from A to B. Whipstitch bottom edge of beak base to top edge of breast, then align this assembled piece to body pieces, matching points B and C; Whipstitch together.

2. Whipstitch sides of tail top to body pieces from green arrow to red arrow. Align tail back with back of body, matching blue dots, then Whipstitch tail back to body and tail top, going up one side, across top and down remaining side.

3. Whipstitch base to bottom edges of breast, sides and tail back.

4. Whipstitch lining front and back to lining sides where indicated. Insert lining inside body, matching points A and blue and green arrows; Whipstitch together. *Note: Bottom edges of lining are not attached to base.* Front and back lining pieces may bow slightly.

5. Use wire cutters to remove shanks from buttons, then glue on buttons for eyes where indicated on graph. Glue wings in place as in photo. ✂

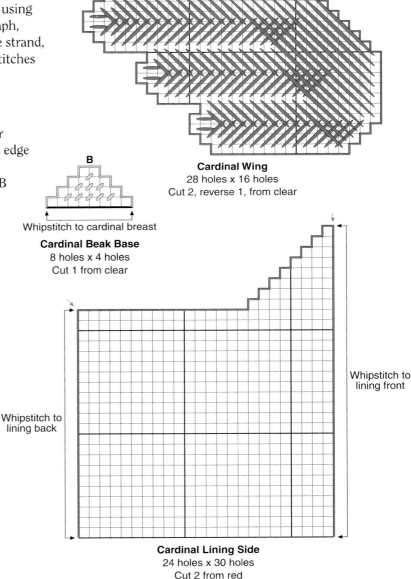

Cardinal Wing
28 holes x 16 holes
Cut 2, reverse 1, from clear

Whipstitch to cardinal breast

Cardinal Beak Base
8 holes x 4 holes
Cut 1 from clear

Whipstitch to lining front

Whipstitch to lining back

Cardinal Lining Side
24 holes x 30 holes
Cut 2 from red

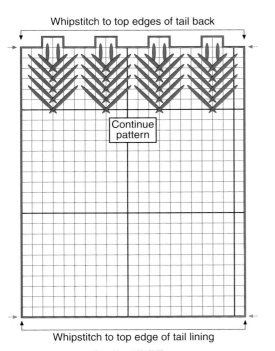

Whipstitch to top edges of tail back

Continue pattern

Whipstitch to top edge of tail lining

Cardinal Tail Top
21 holes x 27 holes
Cut 1 from clear

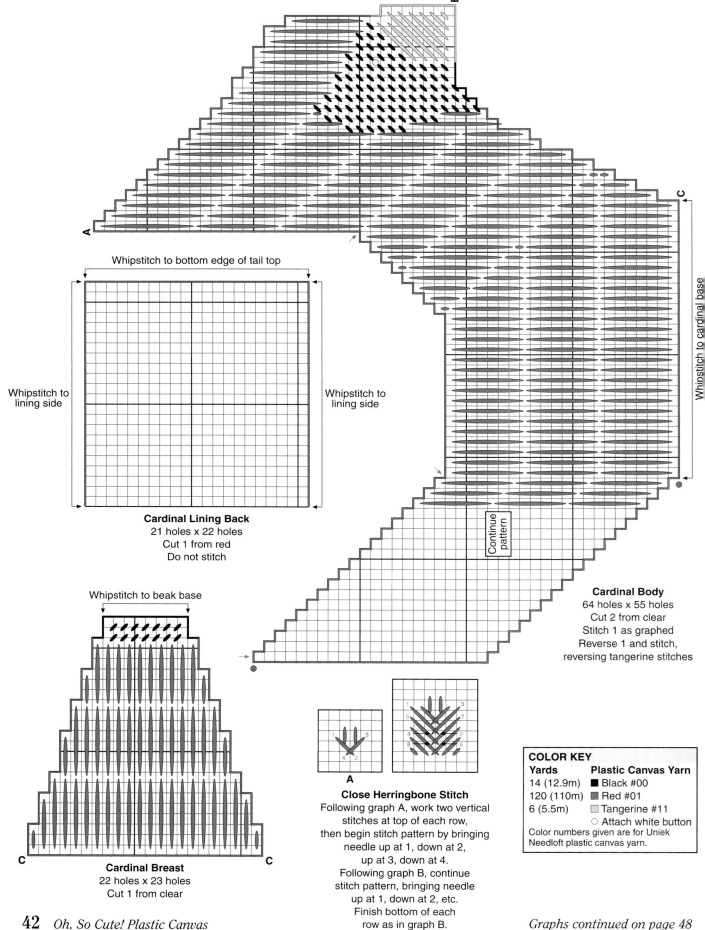

Whipstitch to bottom edge of tail top

Whipstitch to lining side

Whipstitch to lining side

Whipstitch to cardinal base

Cardinal Lining Back
21 holes x 22 holes
Cut 1 from red
Do not stitch

Whipstitch to beak base

Continue pattern

Cardinal Body
64 holes x 55 holes
Cut 2 from clear
Stitch 1 as graphed
Reverse 1 and stitch,
reversing tangerine stitches

Cardinal Breast
22 holes x 23 holes
Cut 1 from clear

A

Close Herringbone Stitch
Following graph A, work two vertical
stitches at top of each row,
then begin stitch pattern by bringing
needle up at 1, down at 2,
up at 3, down at 4.
Following graph B, continue
stitch pattern, bringing needle
up at 1, down at 2, etc.
Finish bottom of each
row as in graph B.

COLOR KEY
Yards	Plastic Canvas Yarn
14 (12.9m)	■ Black #00
120 (110m)	■ Red #01
6 (5.5m)	☐ Tangerine #11
	○ Attach white button

Color numbers given are for Uniek
Needloft plastic canvas yarn.

Graphs continued on page 48

Tiny Treasures

Stitch this tiny box emblazoned with a truck to delight a special son or grandson. Mini cars or other small toys fit nicely inside.

Design by Patricia Klesh

Skill Level

Beginner

Size

4¾ inches W x 1⅞ inches H x 3 inches D
(12.1 cm x 4.8cm x 7.6cm)

Materials

- 1 sheet 7-count plastic canvas
- Worsted weight yarn as listed in color key
- #16 tapestry needle

Instructions

1. Cut plastic canvas according to graphs (this page and page 55).

2. Stitch pieces following graphs, working uncoded areas with light blue Continental Stitches.

3. When background stitching is completed, use 4 plies white and two plies black and yellow yarn to work embroidery.

4. Using light blue through step 5, Whipstitch box sides to box ends, then Whipstitch sides and ends to box base. Overcast top edges.

5. Whipstitch lid long sides to lid short sides, then Whipstitch sides to lid top. Overcast bottom edges. ✄

COLOR KEY	
Yards	**Worsted Weight Yarn**
7 (6.5m)	■ Dark blue
3 (2.8m)	□ White
2 (1.9m)	■ Black
1 (1m)	■ Red
1 (1m)	■ Gray
36 (33m)	Uncoded areas are light blue Continental Stitches
	⁄ Light blue Overcasting and Whipstitching
	⁄ White (4-ply) Straight Stitch
	⁄ Black (2-ply) Backstitch
	⁄ Yellow (2-ply) Running Stitch

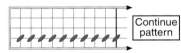

Tiny Treasures Lid Long Side
31 holes x 4 holes
Cut 2

Tiny Treasures Lid Short Side
19 holes x 4 holes
Cut 2

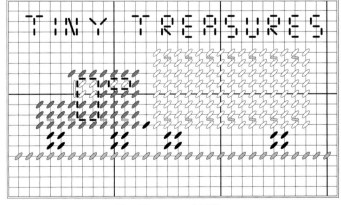

Tiny Treasures Lid Top
31 holes x 19 holes
Cut 1

Graphs continued on page 55

Graphs continued on page 55

Strawberry Dollhouse & Furniture

Hours of fun await your special little girl when you present her with a sweet dollhouse filled with miniature furniture! Designs by Janna Britton

Skill Level
Intermediate

Size
House: 7¾ inches W x 10¾ inches H x 3¼ inches D (19.7cm x 27.3cm x 8.3cm), including handle

Bed: 3⅜ inches W x 5¼ inches L x 3⅜ inches H (8.6cm x 13.3cm x 8.6cm), including leaf

Chair: 1¾ inches W x 3⅜ inches H x 1⅝ inches D (4.4cm x 8.6cm x 4.1cm), including leaf

Stool: 2 inches W x 2¼ inches H x 2¼ inches D (5.1cm x 5.7cm x 5.7cm), including leaf

Materials
- 4 sheets red 7-count plastic canvas
- 2 sheets green 7-count plastic canvas
- 1 sheet pastel yellow 7-count plastic canvas
- Uniek Needloft plastic canvas yarn as listed in color key
- #16 tapestry needle
- 2 sheets red adhesive-backed felt
- 5½ x 6-inch (14 x 15.2cm) piece green felt
- 3 (1-inch) squares hook-and-loop tape
- Tulip dandelion yellow #65301 dimensional matte paint from Duncan Enterprises
- Small paintbrush
- Hot-glue gun

Dollhouse

1. Following graphs throughout (pages 46, 47 and 48), cut front, back, sides and base from red plastic canvas. Cut leaf flap, top, handle pieces and door window from green plastic canvas, cutting away blue areas. Cut door and house windows from pastel yellow plastic canvas, cutting away blue areas.

2. Cut two pieces red felt slightly smaller all around than front and back. Set aside.

3. Place door and house windows on front where indicated with yellow shading. Stitch in place with yellow following graphs, working through both layers of canvas.

4. Place door window on door along green highlighted lines. Stitch in place with Christmas green yarn, working through all three layers.

5. Stitch dollhouse front, back, sides, top and base following graphs, stitching around door and windows on front. Stitch flap and one handle piece, following graphs. Do not stitch remaining handle piece.

6. Overcast around side and top edges of front from blue dot to blue dot. Overcast around side and bottom edges of flap from blue dot to blue dot. Whipstitch stitched handle to unstitched handle along long edges.

7. Whipstitch sides to base, then Whipstitch sides and base to back, easing as necessary to fit. Whipstitch top to back, then Whipstitch top to sides, Whipstitching handles in place where indicated while stitching. Front edges of sides will remain unstitched.

8. Whipstitch remaining edges of top and flap together. Whipstitch bottom edge of front to base.

Bed

1. Following graphs throughout (pages 46, 47 and 48), cut headboard and footboard from red plastic canvas; cut stems and bed sides from green plastic canvas. Also cut two 31-hole x 15-hole pieces from green for bed mattress.

2. Stitch headboard and footboard pieces following graphs, leaving area below top blue line on inner headboard unworked and shaded pink area on inner footboard unworked.

3. Stitch and Overcast stems. Stitch bed sides as graphed. Mattress pieces will remain unstitched.

4. Whipstitch mattress pieces to top and bottom edges of sides, forming a rectangular box. Using Christmas red, Whipstitch ends of mattress pieces to blue lines on inner headboard and footboard pieces, working over previous stitches on footboard where necessary.

5. Whipstitch headboard pieces together, attaching ends of bed sides where indicated while Whipstitching. Whipstitch footboard pieces together.

6. Using Christmas green, tack headboard stem and footboard stems in place along top edges (see photo).

Chair

1. Following graphs throughout (pages 46 and 47), cut chair back pieces from red plastic canvas; cut chair seat, front legs, side legs and stem from green plastic canvas.

2. Stitch and Overcast stem. Stitch chair back pieces, working red stitches only at this time. Stitch seat, front legs and side legs.

3. Whipstitch wrong sides of chair backs together around side and top edges from arrow to arrow, then with back of chair facing up, stitch Christmas green Continental Stitches and Reverse Continental Stitches on legs.

4. Using Christmas green through step 5, Whipstitch seat to top edges of leg sides and front, then Whipstitch seat to chair back along blue line, working over previous stitching.

5. Whipstitch four corners of legs together; Whipstitch edges of back legs together from blue dot to blue dot. Do not stitch remaining edges of chair legs.

6. Using Christmas green, tack stem in place along top edge (see photo).

Table

1. Following graphs (pages 47 and 48) throughout, cut front, back and side/top from red plastic canvas; cut stem from green plastic canvas. Also cut one 6-hole x 9-hole piece from red plastic canvas for stool base. Base will remain unstitched.

2. Stitch and Overcast stem. Stitch front, back and side/top.

3. Whipstitch unstitched base to ends of side/top piece. Whipstitch front and back to side/top, easing as necessary to fit. Whipstitch front and back to base.

4. Using Christmas green, tack stem in place on top of table (see photo).

Finishing

1. Paint small seed dots on furniture and back of house with dandelion yellow paint and paintbrush. Allow to dry.

2. Adhere red felt to wrong sides of dollhouse front and back. Fold green felt to fit

bed, folding back top edge to form pillow. If desired, steam with iron to set side folds.

3. Adhere hook-and-loop tape squares under leaf points on flap and to dollhouse front. ✂

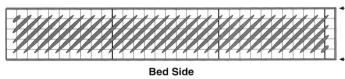

Whipstitch to headboard

Bed Side
31 holes x 5 holes
Cut 2, reverse 1, from green

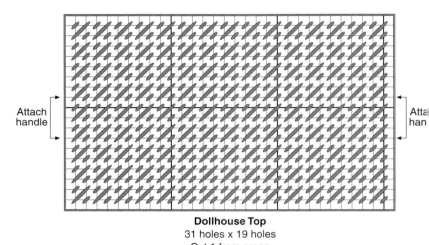

Attach handle →

← Attach handle

Dollhouse Top
31 holes x 19 holes
Cut 1 from green

COLOR KEY

Yards	Plastic Canvas Yarn
131 (119.8m)	■ Christmas red #02
42 (38.4m)	■ Christmas green #28
6 (5.5m)	☐ Yellow #57
	╱ Christmas green #28 Backstitch and Straight Stitch
	╱ Yellow #57 Backstitch and Straight Stitch

Color numbers given are for Uniek Needloft plastic canvas yarn.

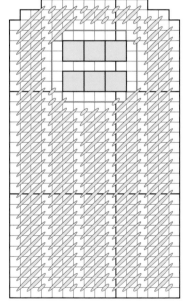

Dollhouse Door
16 holes x 29 holes
Cut 1 from pastel yellow,
cutting away blue areas

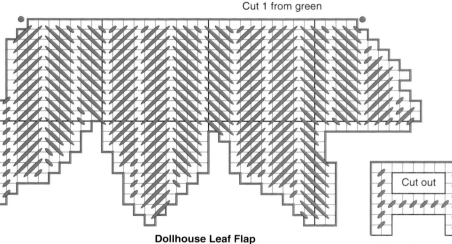

Dollhouse Leaf Flap
40 holes x 20 holes
Cut 1 from green

Cut out

Chair Side Legs
9 holes x 7 holes
Cut 2 from green

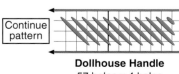

Continue pattern

Dollhouse Handle
57 holes x 4 holes
Cut 2 from green
Stitch 1

Footboard Stem
9 holes x 7 holes
Cut 2 from green

Chair Stem
9 holes x 7 holes
Cut 1 from green

Chair Seat
9 holes x 8 holes
Cut 1 from green

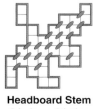

Headboard Stem
8 holes x 8 holes
Cut 1 from green

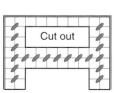

Cut out

Chair Front Legs
10 holes x 7 holes
Cut 1 from green

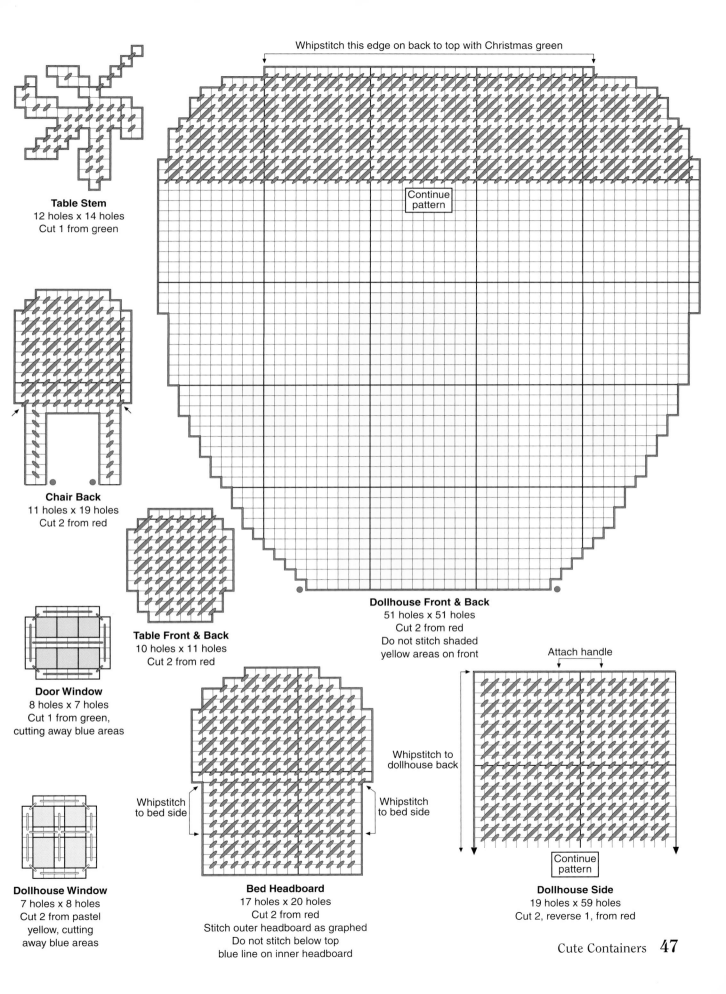

Table Stem
12 holes x 14 holes
Cut 1 from green

Chair Back
11 holes x 19 holes
Cut 2 from red

Door Window
8 holes x 7 holes
Cut 1 from green,
cutting away blue areas

Dollhouse Window
7 holes x 8 holes
Cut 2 from pastel
yellow, cutting
away blue areas

Table Front & Back
10 holes x 11 holes
Cut 2 from red

Whipstitch this edge on back to top with Christmas green

Continue
pattern

Dollhouse Front & Back
51 holes x 51 holes
Cut 2 from red
Do not stitch shaded
yellow areas on front

Whipstitch
to bed side

Whipstitch
to bed side

Bed Headboard
17 holes x 20 holes
Cut 2 from red
Stitch outer headboard as graphed
Do not stitch below top
blue line on inner headboard

Attach handle

Whipstitch to
dollhouse back

Continue
pattern

Dollhouse Side
19 holes x 59 holes
Cut 2, reverse 1, from red

Cute Containers 47

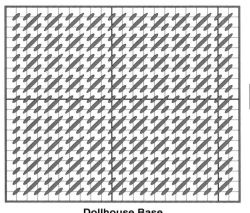

Dollhouse Base
22 holes x 19 holes
Cut 1 from red

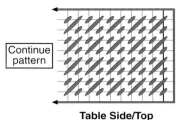

Continue pattern

Table Side/Top
31 holes x 9 holes
Cut 1 from red

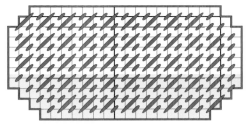

Bed Footboard
22 holes x 11 holes
Cut 2 from red
Stitch outer footboard as graphed
Do not stitch shaded pink
area on inner footboard

Regal Cardinal

Continued from page 42

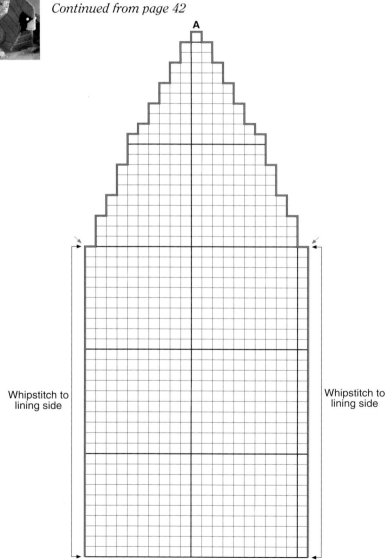

A

Whipstitch to lining side

Whipstitch to lining side

Cardinal Lining Front
21 holes x 51 holes
Cut 1 from red

Whipstitch to top edges of tail top

Continue pattern

Whipstitch to cardinal base

Cardinal Tail Back
21 holes x 50 holes
Cut 1 from clear

Sewing Notions Catch-All

Keep your bobbins and other sewing notions handy with this nifty little button-embellished tote. Design by Ronda Bryce

Skill Level
Intermediate

Size
5¼ inches H x 4¼ inches in diameter (10.8cm x 11.4cm)

Materials
- 2 sheets clear 7-count plastic canvas
- Small amount red 7-count plastic canvas
- 2 (4-inch) Uniek QuickShape plastic canvas radial circles
- 2 (3-inch) Uniek QuickShape plastic canvas radial circles
- Coats & Clark Red Heart Classic worsted weight yarn Art. E267 as listed in color key
- Coats & Clark Red Heart Super Saver worsted weight yarn Art. E300 as listed in color key
- #16 tapestry needle
- 21 buttons in various sizes: red, green, blue, yellow and orange
- Hand-sewing needle
- Blue and beige sewing thread
- Hot-glue gun

Catch-All
1. Cut catch-all side from clear plastic canvas following graph (page 50). Cut two outermost rows of holes from one 4-inch plastic canvas radial circle for catch-all base. Base will remain unstitched.

2. Stitch catch-all side as graphed. Using black throughout, Whipstitch side edges together, then Overcast top edge; Whipstitch bottom edge to unstitched base.

Flat Spools
1. Cut six flat spools from clear plastic canvas according to graph (page 50).

2. Stitch and Overcast two flat spools as graphed and one each replacing cherry red with vibrant orange, emerald, skipper blue and bright yellow.

3. Using hand-sewing needle and beige thread, sew button desired to each spool where indicated on graph.

4. Using camel yarn, tack spools together where indicated with brackets, forming a circle.

5. Slip circle of spools down over catch-all side until bottom edges are even.

Lid

1. Cut lid side from clear plastic canvas according to graph (page 54).

2. Stitch lid side and lid top following graphs, working uncoded areas on lid side with bright yellow Continental Stitches and leaving shaded blue area on lid top unworked.

3. Whipstitch side edges of lid sides together with black. Using red, Overcast bottom edge of lid side, then Whipstitch top edge to lid top.

Round Spool

1. Following graphs (this page and page 54), cut round spool from red plastic canvas and two spool ends from 3-inch plastic canvas radial circles, cutting away gray areas.

2. Stitch pieces following graphs. Whipstitch side edges of spool together; Overcast top and bottom edges. stitch and Overcast round spool ends.

3. Using sewing needle and beige thread, center and stitch ends to top and bottom edges of spool, then stitch spool to center of lid.

4. Using sewing needle and blue thread, stitch buttons to lid (see photo). ✂

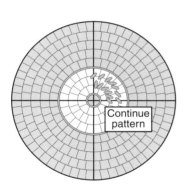

Flat Spool
14 holes x 16 holes
Cut 6 from clear
Stitch 2 as graphed and
1 each replacing cherry red
with vibrant orange, emerald,
skipper blue and bright yellow

Continue pattern

COLOR KEY

Yards	Worsted Weight Yarn
3 (2.8m)	■ Black #312
16 (14.7)	▨ Cherry red #319
8 (7.4m)	▨ Warm brown #336
3 (2.8m)	Vibrant orange #354
3 (2.8m)	Emerald #676
10 (9.2m)	▨ Skipper blue #848
12 (11m)	Uncoded areas on lid side are bright yellow #324 Continental Stitches
	╱ Black #312 Backstitch
	╱ Cherry red #319 Straight Stitch
	○ Attach button

Color numbers given are for Coats & Clark Red Heart Classic worsted weight yarn Art. E267 and Super Saver worsted weight yarn Art. E300.

Catch-All Side
78 holes x 23 holes
Cut 1 from clear

Continue pattern

Round Spool End
Cut 2 from
3-inch radial circles,
cutting away gray areas

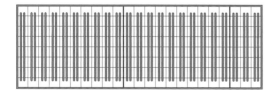

Round Spool
23 holes x 8 holes
Cut 1 from red

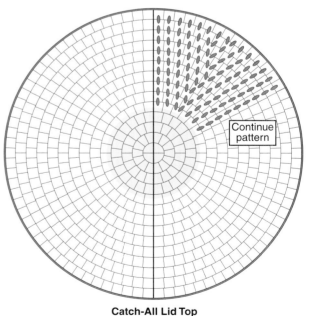

Catch-All Lid Top
Stitch 1 (4-inch) radial circle
Do not stitch
shaded blue area

Graphs continued on page 54

Apple Coffee Can Covers

Empty coffee cans become stylish storage pieces when fitted with stitched covers featuring an apple motif. Designs by Angie Arickx

Skill Level
Beginner

Size
Large Cover: 7 inches H x 5½ inches in diameter (17.8 cm x 14cm) Fits 26-ounce coffee can
Small Cover: 5¾ inches H x 4¼ inches in diameter (14.6 cm x 10.8cm) Fits 11.5-ounce coffee can

Materials
- 1 artist-size sheet soft 7-count plastic canvas
- 2 (6-inch) Uniek QuickShape plastic canvas radial circles
- 2 (4-inch) Uniek QuickShape plastic canvas radial circles
- Uniek Needloft plastic canvas yarn as listed in color key
- #16 tapestry needle
- 26-ounce empty coffee can
- 11.5-ounce empty coffee can
- Heavy book or other weighted object
- Craft glue (suitable for plastic)

Instructions
1. Cut apples and cover cylinders from plastic canvas according to graphs (pages 52, 53 and 54).

2. For large cover, cut the two outermost rows of holes from one 6-inch plastic canvas radial circle for lid cover and one outermost row of holes from remaining 6-inch circle for base.

3. For small cover, cut one outermost row of holes from one 4-inch plastic canvas radial circle for lid cover. Leave second 4-inch circle as is for base.

4. Using eggshell, Continental Stitch around circles for lid covers, leaving two or three center rows unworked; Overcast edges. Do not stitch bases.

5. Following graphs throughout stitching, stitch and Overcast apples, working uncoded areas with burgundy Continental Stitches.

6. Stitch cylinders, working uncoded areas with eggshell Continental Stitches and overlapping two rows of holes as indicated before completing stitching.

7. Whipstitch cylinders to corresponding bases. Overcast top edges.

8. Glue lid covers to corresponding plastic coffee can lids. Place lids on cans and rest heavy book or object on top until glue dries. Center and glue one apple to corresponding lid. Allow to dry.

9. Insert cans in covers. ✂

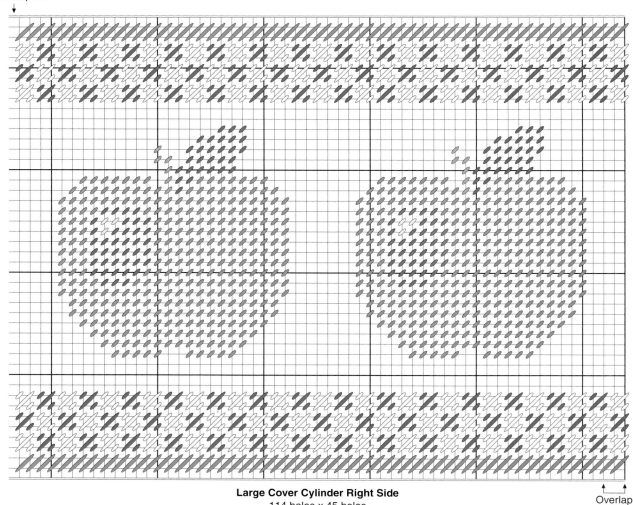

Center Row
Do not repeat

Large Cover Cylinder Right Side
114 holes x 45 holes
Cut 1
Join with left side before cutting

Overlap

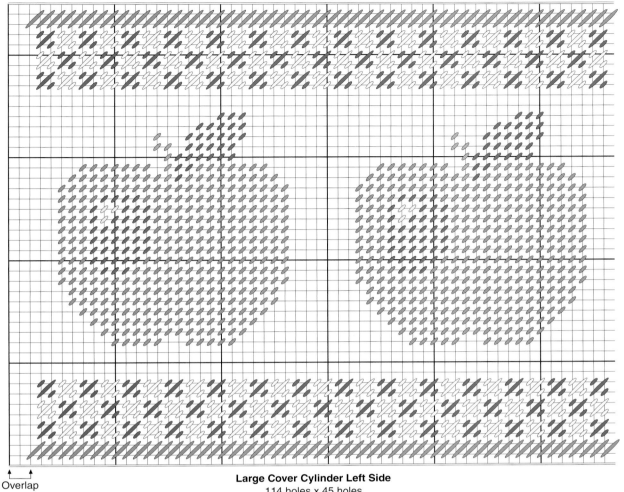

Overlap

Large Cover Cylinder Left Side
114 holes x 45 holes
Cut 1
Join with right side before cutting

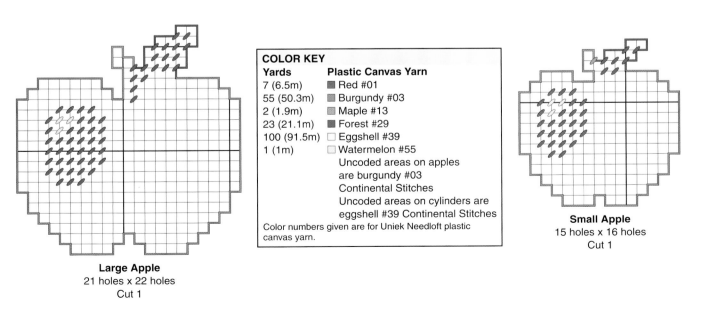

Large Apple
21 holes x 22 holes
Cut 1

COLOR KEY

Yards	Plastic Canvas Yarn
7 (6.5m)	Red #01
55 (50.3m)	Burgundy #03
2 (1.9m)	Maple #13
23 (21.1m)	Forest #29
100 (91.5m)	Eggshell #39
1 (1m)	Watermelon #55

Uncoded areas on apples
are burgundy #03
Continental Stitches
Uncoded areas on cylinders are
eggshell #39 Continental Stitches

Color numbers given are for Uniek Needloft plastic
canvas yarn.

Small Apple
15 holes x 16 holes
Cut 1

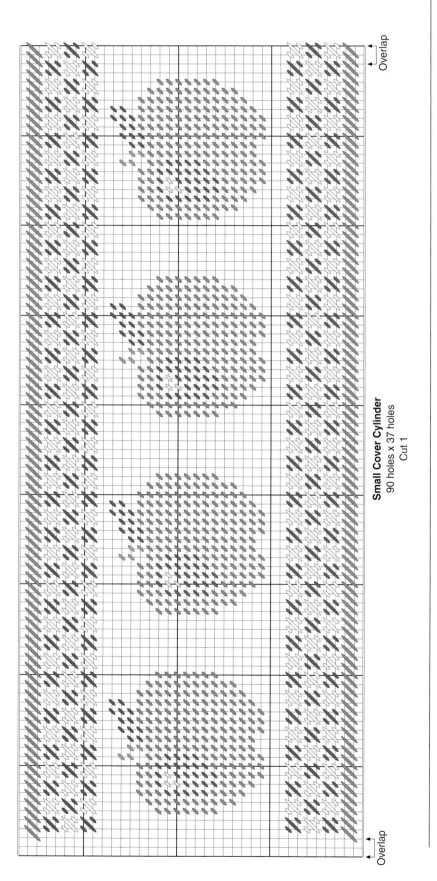

Small Cover Cylinder
90 holes x 37 holes
Cut 1

Overlap

Overlap

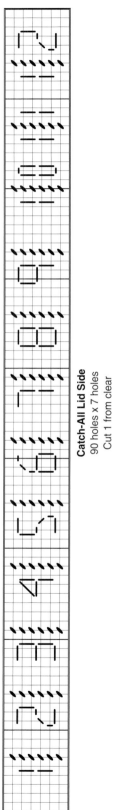

Catch-All Lid Side
90 holes x 7 holes
Cut 1 from clear

Tiny Treasures

Continued from page 43

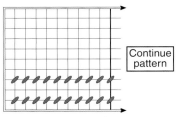

Tiny Treasures Box Side
29 holes x 10 holes
Cut 2

Tiny Treasures Box End
17 holes x 10 holes
Cut 2

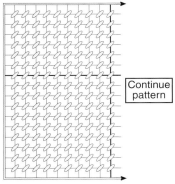

Tiny Treasures Box Base
29 holes x 17 holes
Cut 1

Mini Butterfly Tote

Continued from page 30

COLOR KEY

Yards	Plastic Canvas Yarn
3 (2.8m)	■ Black #00
4 (3.7m)	□ White #41
4 (3.7m)	▨ Bright orange #58
7 (6.5m)	□ Bright yellow #63
25 (22.9m)	▨ Bright purple #64
	Uncoded areas are bright purple #64 Continental Stitches
	● Attach wire antennae

Color numbers given are for Uniek Needloft plastic canvas yarn.

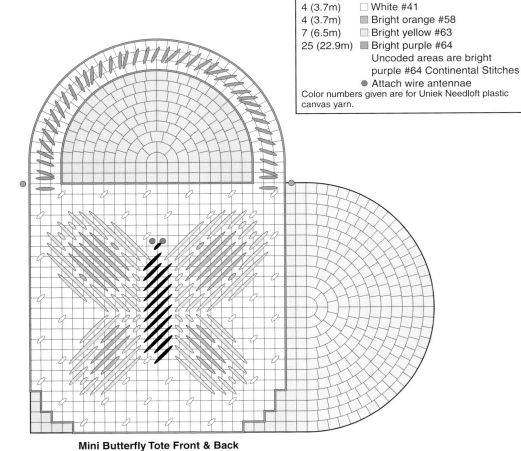

Mini Butterfly Tote Side
12 holes x 26 holes
Cut 2

Mini Butterfly Tote Front & Back
Cut 2 from plastic canvas hearts,
cutting away gray areas

I see the Moon
and the Moon sees me
God bless the Moon
and God bless me!

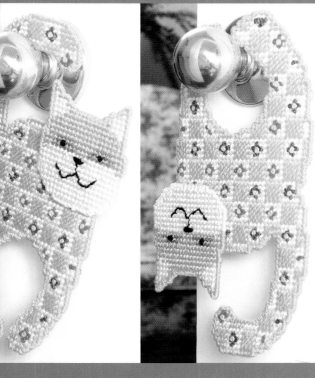

Whimsical Home Accents

Decorate your home with fun wall art created with yarn and 7-count plastic canvas. Fun and whimsy fill this fabulous chapter!

Time for Fall Turkey Set

Stitched with novelty yarn and embellished with silk autumn leaves, this friendly pair will add cheer to your home during the autumn months! Designs by Laura Victory

Skill Level
Intermediate

Size
Large Turkey: 10¾ inches W x 12 inches H (27.3cm x 30.5cm), excluding hanger

Small Turkey: 8½ inches W x 9 inches H (21.6cm x 22.9cm)

Materials
- ¼ sheet 7-count plastic canvas
- 2 (3-inch/7.6cm) plastic canvas radial circles
- 4-inch/10.2cm plastic canvas radial circle
- 6-inch/15.2cm plastic canvas radial circle
- Uniek Needloft plastic canvas yarn as listed in color key
- Spinrite Bernat Boa feather yarn as listed in color key
- #16 tapestry needle
- 2 (10mm) movable eyes
- 2 (15mm) movable eyes
- Artificial maple leaves in autumn colors
- 3¾ inches (9.5cm) magnet strip
- 1 yard (1m) 2-inch/5.1cm-wide ribbon to match leaves and yarn
- Hand-sewing needle and sewing thread to match ribbon
- Hot-glue gun

Instructions

1. Cut beaks and legs/feet from plastic canvas according to graphs (page 60).

2. Following graphs throughout, stitch and Overcast beaks and legs/feet with tangerine. For heads, stitch and Overcast 3-inch/7.6 radial circles with camel.

3. For bodies, Backstitch and Overcast 4-inch/10.2cm and 6-inch/15.2cm plastic canvas radial circles with phoenix, working around each row of holes.

4. Using photo as a guide, glue heads to front tops of corresponding bodies. Glue legs/feet to bottom back sides.

5. Glue 10mm movable eyes and one beak to head of small turkey; glue 15mm movable eyes and remaining beak to head of large turkey.

6. For turkey feathers, glue artificial autumn leaves to backs of turkey bodies and heads.

7. Cut magnet strip into three pieces and glue to back of small turkey.

8. Using hand-sewing needle and sewing thread, work a running stitch along one edge at center 18-inches (45.7cm) of ribbon. Pull slightly to gather, making a circle large enough to hang over doorknob. Glue ribbon tails to back of large turkey.

9. Hang large turkey on wall or over doorknob. ✂

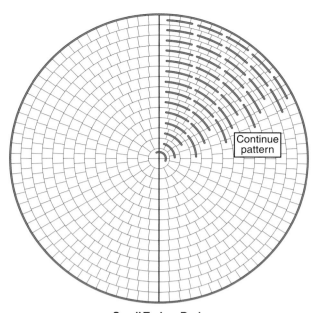

Small Turkey Body
Stitch 1, using
4-inch/10.2cm radial circle

Turkey Head
Stitch 1 for each head,
using 3-inch/7.6cm radial circle

Large Turkey Leg/Foot
8 holes x 23 holes
Cut 2

Small Turkey Leg/Foot
5 holes x 14 holes
Cut 2

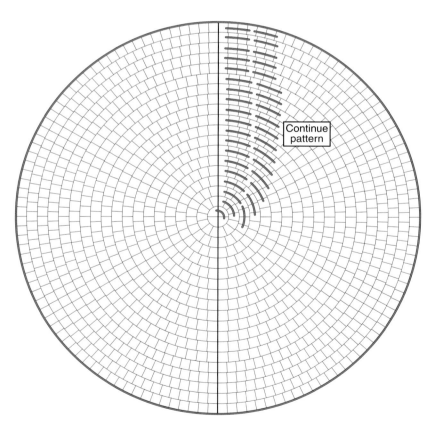

Large Turkey Body
Stitch 1, using
6-inch/15.2cm radial circle

COLOR KEY		
Yards	**Plastic Canvas Yarn**	
5 (4.6m)	☐ Tangerine #11	
9 (8.3m)	☐ Camel #43	
	╱ Tangerine #11 Backstitch and Straight Stitch	
	Feather Yarn	
27 (24.7m)	╱ Phoenix #81505 Backstitch and Overcasting	

Color numbers given are for Uniek Needloft plastic canvas yarn and Spinrite Bernat Boa feather yarn.

Turkey Beak
5 holes x 4 holes
Cut 1 for each turkey

Peace on Earth

Delicate and serene, stitch this angel with love and add a peaceful accent to your home. Design by Michele Wilcox

Skill Level
Beginner

Size
15 inches W x 7 inches H (38.1cm x 17.8cm), excluding hanger

Materials
- 2 sheets 7-count plastic canvas
- Uniek Needloft plastic canvas yarn as listed in color key
- Uniek Needloft solid metallic craft cord as listed in color key
- #3 pearl cotton as listed in color key
- #16 tapestry needle
- Sheet white adhesive-backed felt
- ½ yard (0.5m) ⅜-inch/1cm-wide blue satin ribbon
- 4½-inch/11.4cm-wide piece cardboard
- Hot-glue gun

Instructions
1. Cut plastic canvas according to graphs (pages 62 and 63). Cut white felt slightly smaller all around than base, excluding tabs.

2. Following graphs throughout, stitch and Overcast wings, reversing one before stitching. Stitch and Overcast remaining pieces, working uncoded background on base with camel Continental Stitches and uncoded background on head with pale peach Continental Stitches.

3. When background stitching is completed, use pearl cotton to embroider facial features on head and snowflakes on base.

4. For hair, wrap cinnamon yarn around 4½-inch/ 11.4cm-wide cardboard 40 times. Slip off cardboard and tie tightly in center of loops with another length of cinnamon yarn. Cut loops and brush with hairbrush to make yarn fuzzy.

5. Using photo as a guide through step 7, center hair on head where indicated on graph, then glue hair in place. Slip halo into hair and glue to secure.

6. Attach felt to back of base. Glue wings, then head to base front.

7. For hanger, thread ends of ribbon from back to front through holes on tabs of base; knot ends. ✂

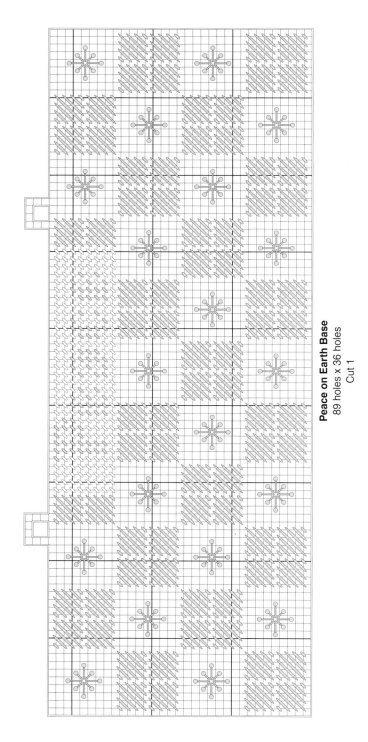

Peace on Earth Base
89 holes x 36 holes
Cut 1

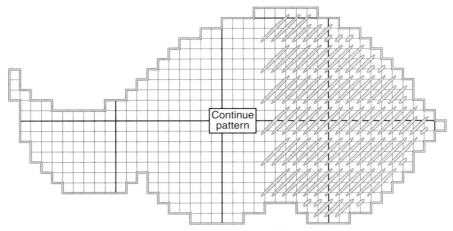

Peace on Earth Angel Wing
41 holes x 21 holes
Cut 2, reverse 1

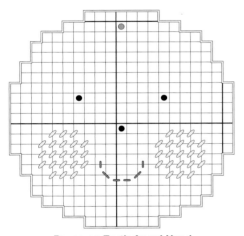

Peace on Earth Angel Head
21 holes x 21 holes
Cut 1

COLOR KEY

Yards	Plastic Canvas Yarn
2 (1.9m)	☐ Pink #07
30 (27.5m)	☐ Sail blue #35
20 (18.3m)	☐ Beige #40
8 (7.4m)	☐ White #41
20 (18.3m)	Uncoded background on base is camel #43 Continental Stitches
9 (8.3m)	Uncoded background on face is pale peach #56 Continental Stitches
	⁄ Pale peach #56 Overcasting
10 (9.2m)	● Attach cinnamon #14 hair
	Solid Metallic Craft Cord
3 (2.8m)	☐ Solid gold #20
	#3 Pearl Cotton
16 (14.7m)	⁄ White Straight Stitch
1 (1m)	⁄ Red Backstitch
1 (1m)	● Black French Knot
	○ White French Knot

Color numbers given are for Uniek Needloft plastic canvas yarn and solid metallic craft cord.

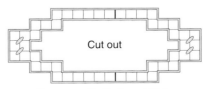

Peace on Earth Angel Halo
18 holes x 7 holes
Cut 1

Bluebird Welcome

Nestled in pretty flowers and decorated with wire, this little bluebird adds pretty spring color wherever he roosts. Design by Kathy Wirth

Skill Level
Beginner

Size
8½ inches W x 8½ inches H (21.6cm x 21.6cm)

Materials
- 1 sheet 7-count plastic canvas
- Uniek Needloft plastic canvas yarn as listed in color key
- #3 pearl cotton as listed in color key
- #16 tapestry needle
- #18 tapestry needle

- 24 inches (61cm) 24-gauge black Fun Wire from Amoco
- ⅛-inch (0.3cm) dowel or large nail
- Wire cutters
- Picture hanger
- Hot-glue gun

Project Note

Use #16 tapestry needle with yarn and #18 tapestry needle with pearl cotton.

Instructions

1. Cut plastic canvas according to graphs (this page and page 66).

2. Stitch and Overcast piece following graphs, working uncoded background on nest with beige Continental Stitches.

3. When background stitching and Overcasting are completed, work embroidery with black pearl cotton on body, nest and flowers. Work Straight Stitch in center of beak and two French Knots for eyes.

4. Place beak on head where indicated with yellow highlighting. Using black pearl cotton, attach beak to head with Straight Stitches over corners, then work French Knots on head at beak corners.

5. Using photo as a guide through step 6, glue head and feet to bird; glue flowers to nest.

6. Cut wire into two equal lengths, Wrap end of one length around top edge of one flower, leaving a 2-inch (5.1cm) tail. Curl tail and rest of wire around dowel or nail. Insert other end of wire through tip of wing, wrapping around edge and leaving a tail.

7. Repeat with remaining length of wire on other side of bird and nest. Adjust coils as desired, trimming wire tails as needed. To secure, glue back of pieces where wire is inserted.

8. Glue or stitch picture hanger to top back of bird body. ✂

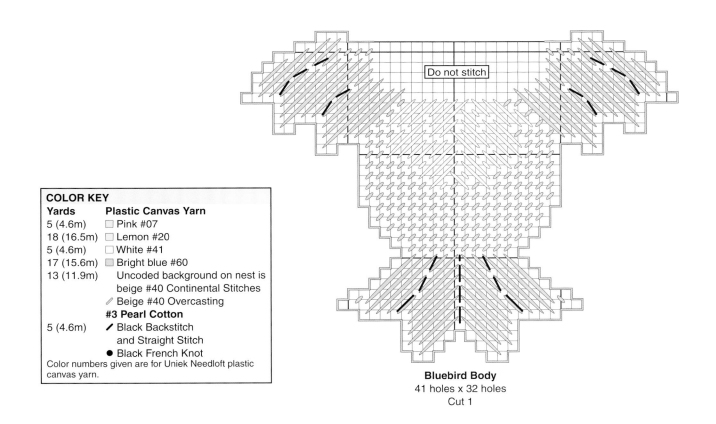

COLOR KEY

Yards	Plastic Canvas Yarn
5 (4.6m)	☐ Pink #07
18 (16.5m)	☐ Lemon #20
5 (4.6m)	☐ White #41
17 (15.6m)	☐ Bright blue #60
13 (11.9m)	Uncoded background on nest is beige #40 Continental Stitches
	╱ Beige #40 Overcasting
	#3 Pearl Cotton
5 (4.6m)	╱ Black Backstitch and Straight Stitch
	● Black French Knot

Color numbers given are for Uniek Needloft plastic canvas yarn.

Do not stitch

Bluebird Body
41 holes x 32 holes
Cut 1

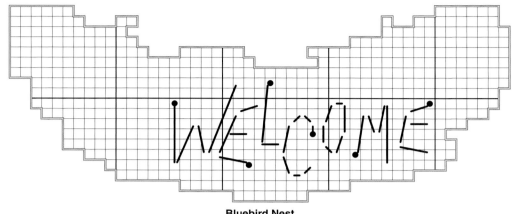

Bluebird Nest
47 holes x 19 holes
Cut 1

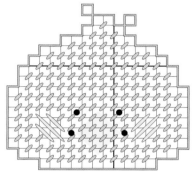

Bluebird Head
17 holes x 16 holes
Cut 1

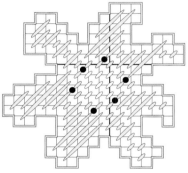

Bluebird Welcome Pink Flower
17 holes x 16 holes
Cut 1

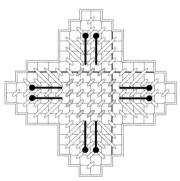

Bluebird Welcome White Flower
16 holes x 16 holes
Cut 1

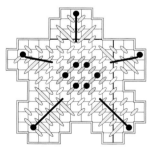

Bluebird Welcome Yellow Flower
13 holes x 13 holes
Cut 1

Bluebird Beak
3 holes x 3 holes
Cut 1

Bluebird Foot
8 holes x 8 holes
Cut 2

Quilting Bee

Stitch, stitch, stitch! This adorable little bee will be right at home in your sewing room or will make a wonderful gift for a dear friend.

Design by Janelle Giese

Skill Level
Advanced

Size
9 inches W x 10½ inches H (22.9cm x 26.7cm)

Materials
- ⅔ sheet 7-count plastic canvas
- Coats & Clark Red Heart Classic worsted weight yarn

Art. E267 as listed in color key
- Kreinik Tapestry (#12) Braid as listed in color key
- #3 pearl cotton as listed in color key
- #5 pearl cotton as listed in color key
- DMC 6-strand embroidery floss as listed in color key
- #16 tapestry needle
- 1¼ inch/3.2cm-long gold eye pin
- Sawtooth hanger
- Hot-glue gun

Project Notes

The diamond, heart, pentagon, star, square, triangle and inverted triangle shapes designate Continental Stitches.

When working tan portions of partial Smyrna Cross Stitches and when Backstitching wings with vintage gold braid, pierce centers of underlying eggshell Cross Stitches.

Instructions

1. Cut plastic canvas according to graph.

2. Work background stitches and Overcast piece following graph. When working Smyrna Cross Stitches on wings, work eggshell Cross Stitches first as the base stitch, then work tan full and partial Upright Cross Stitches on top following graph and Project Notes.

3. Using full strand of yarn throughout, work black Straight Stitches for eyes and eggshell Straight Stitches for eye highlights. Work copper Backstitches on quilt.

4. Using 2 plies dark antique mauve floss, Backstitch heart shapes for cheeks and Lazy Daisy Stitches for lips.

5. Work black pearl cotton embroidery, then work vintage gold braid Backstitches on wings (see Project Notes) and Running Stitches on quilt.

6. Referring to graph for placement, slide eye pin (shown in red) through yarn on thumb. Attach one end of "thread" by drawing vintage gold braid down through eye of pin to back side. Secure with a small stitch, then bring back up through eye of pin, allowing tail to hang free.

7. Bring other end of braid (thread) down through hole indicated at thread placement point; secure on back side. Secure pin with a very small dab of glue.

8. Using black #5 pearl cotton, sew sawtooth hanger to center back of piece at top of bee's head. ✂

COLOR KEY	
Yards	**Worsted Weight Yarn**
7 (6.5m)	⊘ Black #12
5 (4.6m)	⊘ Eggshell #111
5 (4.6m)	♡ Cornmeal #220
7 (6.5m)	☆ Maize #261
7 (6.5m)	⊘ Bronze #286
4 (3.7m)	◇ Copper #289
3 (2.8m)	⊘ Tan #334
5 (4.6m)	△ Mid brown #339
1 (1m)	■ Coffee #365
2 (1.9m)	⊘ Light sage #631
1 (1m)	▲ Honey gold #645
1 (1m)	⊘ Cameo rose #759
3 (2.8m)	✶ New berry #760
2 (1.9m)	▼ Country red #914
10 (9.2m)	⬟ Cardinal #917
	Uncoded areas are black #12 Continental Stitches
	⁄ Black #12 Straight Stitch
	⁄ Eggshell #111 Straight Stitch
	⁄ Copper #289 Backstitch
	Tapestry #12 Braid
6 (5.5m)	⁄ Vintage gold #002V Backstitch and Running Stitch
	#3 Pearl Cotton
2 (1.9m)	⁄ Black Backstitch
	● Black French Knot
	#5 Pearl Cotton
6 (5.5m)	⁄ Black Backstitch
	6-Strand Embroidery Floss
1 (1m)	⁄ Dark antique mauve #3726 (2-ply) Backstitch
	⊘ Dark antique mauve #3726 (2-ply) Lazy Daisy Stitch
	● Thread placement point

Color numbers given are for Coats & Clark Red Heart Classic worsted weight yarn Art. E267, Kreinik Tapestry (#12) Braid and DMC 6-strand embroidery floss.

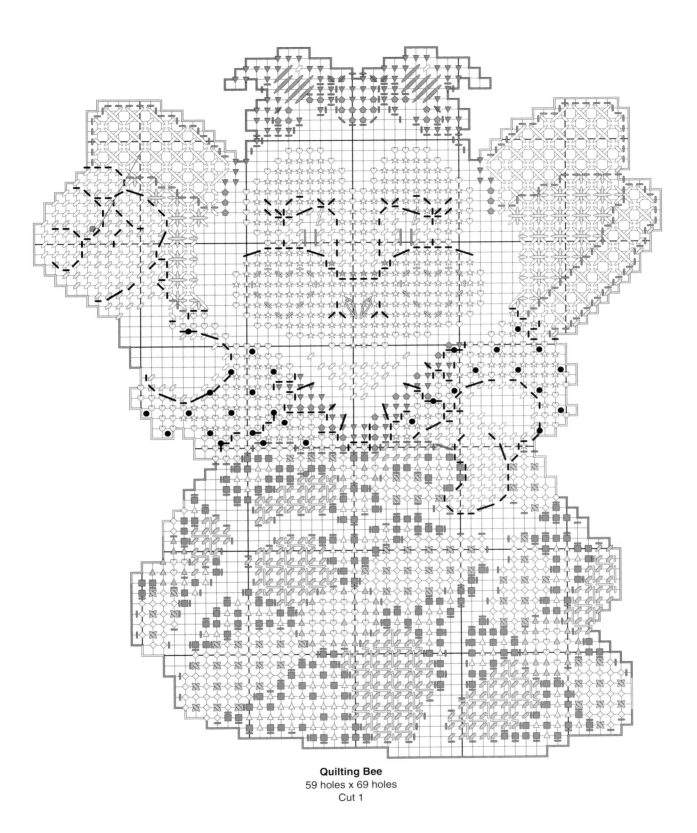

Quilting Bee
59 holes x 69 holes
Cut 1

Topsy-Turvy Cat

Hang this sweet kitty any which way—no matter what, she'll look adorable swinging from your doorknob. Design by Michele Wilcox

Skill Level
Beginner

Size
6 inches W x 9½ inches H (15.2cm x 24.1cm)

Materials
- 1 sheet 7-count plastic canvas
- Uniek Needloft plastic canvas yarn as listed in color key
- #3 pearl cotton as listed in color key
- #16 tapestry needle
- Hot-glue gun

Instructions

1. Cut plastic canvas according to graphs.

2. Stitch and Overcast pieces following graphs, working uncoded backgrounds with eggshell Continental Stitches.

3. When background stitching is completed, use pearl cotton to work red and blue Lazy Daisy Stitches and yellow French Knots on body; use black pearl cotton to Backstitch mouth, Satin Stitch nose and work French Knot eyes.

4. Using photo as a guide, glue head to body. Hang as desired. ✂

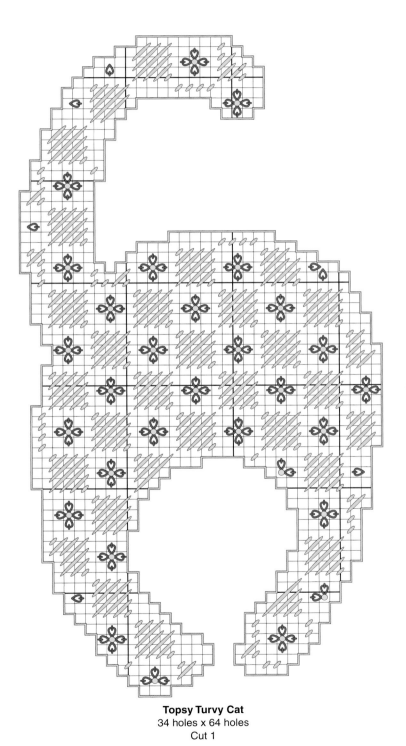

Topsy Turvy Cat
34 holes x 64 holes
Cut 1

COLOR KEY	
Yards	**Plastic Canvas Yarn**
15 (13.8m)	▢ Tangerine #11
1 (1m)	▨ Mermaid #53
18 (16.5m)	Uncoded background is eggshell #39 Continental Stitches
	⁄ Eggshell #39 Overcasting
	#3 Pearl Cotton
1 (1m)	⁄ Black Backstitch and Satin Stitch
5 (4.6m)	ᗡ Red Lazy Daisy Stitch
5 (4.6m)	ᗡ Blue Lazy Daisy Stitch
2 (1.9m)	○ Yellow French Knot
	● Black French Knot

Color numbers given are for Uniek Needloft plastic canvas yarn.

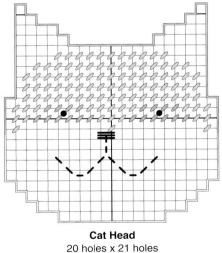

Cat Head
20 holes x 21 holes
Cut 1

Ewes Welcome

Greet your visitors with this whimsical door sign featuring an adorable lamb created just for "ewe." Design by Judy Collishaw

Skill Level
Beginner

Size
5⅜ inches W x 9⅜ inches H (13.7cm x 23.8cm)

Materials
- 1 sheet 7-count plastic canvas
- Worsted weight yarn as listed in color key
- DMC #3 pearl cotton as listed in color key
- DMC #5 pearl cotton as listed in color key
- #16 tapestry needle
- Small fuchsia silk flower with stem
- Hot-glue gun

Instructions
1. Cut plastic canvas according to graphs (this page and page 74).

2. Following graphs through step 6, stitch and Overcast hanger and lamb's head, working uncoded background on hanger with pale yellow Continental Stitches.

3. Following Fig. 1 (page 74), work variation of Turkey Loop Stitches where indicated on head, making stitches ⅜-inch (1cm)-long, moving anchor stitch to adjacent bar available as needed.

4. Stitch lamb's arms and body, working uncoded background on arms with black Continental Stitches. Work variation of Turkey Loop Stitches as instructed in step 3.

5. Overcast arms and body, leaving edges inside brackets unworked.

6. Use two plies yarn to embroider eyes and nose on head and lettering on hanger. Use #3 pearl cotton to embroider mouth and #5 pearl cotton to work embroidery on arms and hanger.

7. Whipstitch arms to body sides along unworked edges.

8. Using photo as a guide, center and glue body just above bottom edge of hanger. Glue head above body at a slight angle. Glue flower stem behind light steel gray Backstitches on arms. ✄

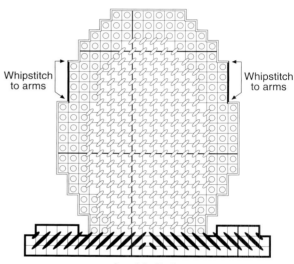

Whipstitch to arms

Whipstitch to arms

Lamb's Body
23 holes x 24 holes
Cut 1

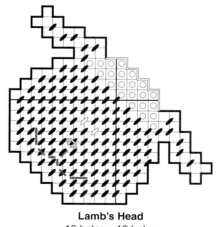

Lamb's Head
19 holes x 19 holes
Cut 1

COLOR KEY

Yards	Worsted Weight Yarn
22 (20.2m)	☐ Pale yellow
17 (15.6m)	☐ Off-white
8 (7.4m)	■ Black
3 (2.8m)	▨ Sage green
2 (1.9m)	☐ White
	Uncoded background on hanger is pale yellow Continental Stitches
	Uncoded background on arms is black Continental Stitches
1 (1m)	⟋ Pink (2-ply) Backstitch
	⟋ Off-white (2-ply) Straight Stitch
	⟋ Sage green (2-ply) Backstitch and Straight Stitch
	○ Off-white Turkey Loop Stitch
	#3 Pearl Cotton
1 (1m)	⟋ Medium rose #899 Backstitch
	#5 Pearl Cotton
1 (1m)	⟋ Light steel gray #318 Backstitch
1 (1m)	⟋ Medium rose #899 Straight Stitch

Color numbers given are for DMC #3 and #5 pearl cotton.

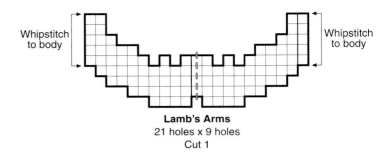

Lamb's Arms
21 holes x 9 holes
Cut 1

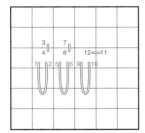

Fig. 1
Turkey Loop Stitch Variation
Bring needle up at 1 and down
at 2 in same hole, creating a loop.
Bring anchor stitch up at 3 and down
over bar at 4, securing stitch.
Continue stitching Turkey Loop
Stitches, moving anchor
stitch as needed to secure.

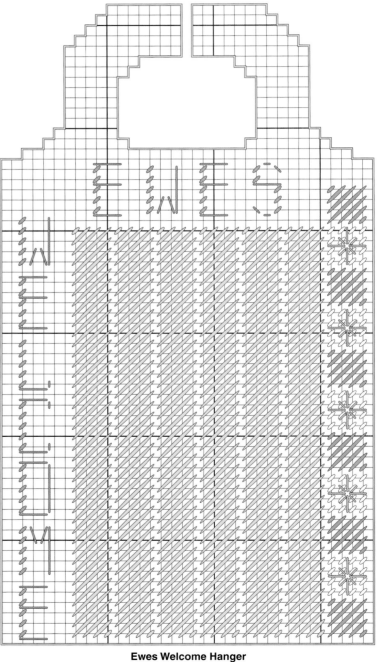

Ewes Welcome Hanger
35 holes x 62 holes
Cut 1

Buzz on in Door Hanger

Make everyone feel right at home with a busy little bee who loves to greet! Design by Deborah Scheblein

Skill Level
Beginner

Size
5⅝ inches W x 11¾ inches H (14.3cm x 29.8cm)

Materials
- ½ sheet 7-count plastic canvas
- Worsted weight yarn as listed in color key
- DMC 6-strand embroidery floss as listed in color key
- #16 tapestry needle
- Small amount black tulle

Instructions
1. Cut plastic canvas according to graph (page 76).

2. Stitch and Overcast piece following graph, working uncoded background with medium blue Continental Stitches.

3. Work Backstitches and Running Stitches with embroidery floss when background stitching and Overcasting are completed.

4. Cut two 1-inch x 2-inch (2.5cm x 5.1cm) strips of black tulle, rounding edges. Thread both strips from back to front through holes indicated on graph. Tie lengths in a tight knot to secure; trim to fit size of bee. ✂

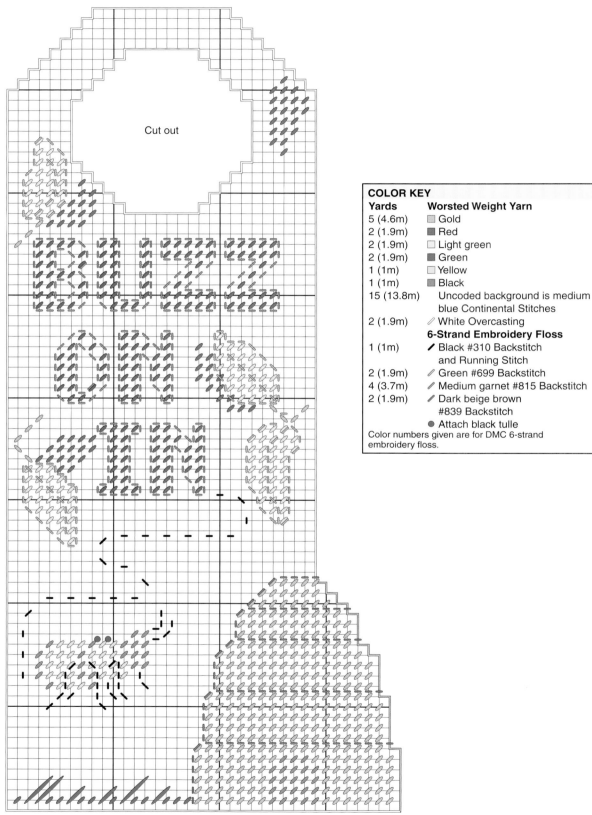

Cut out

COLOR KEY

Yards	Worsted Weight Yarn
5 (4.6m)	Gold
2 (1.9m)	Red
2 (1.9m)	Light green
2 (1.9m)	Green
1 (1m)	Yellow
1 (1m)	Black
15 (13.8m)	Uncoded background is medium blue Continental Stitches
2 (1.9m)	⁄ White Overcasting
	6-Strand Embroidery Floss
1 (1m)	╱ Black #310 Backstitch and Running Stitch
2 (1.9m)	⁄ Green #699 Backstitch
4 (3.7m)	⁄ Medium garnet #815 Backstitch
2 (1.9m)	⁄ Dark beige brown #839 Backstitch
	● Attach black tulle

Color numbers given are for DMC 6-strand embroidery floss.

Buzz on in Door Hanger
37 holes x 78 holes
Cut 1

Ahoy, Matey

Every good pirate never leaves port without his parrot, and this sea-loving fellow is no exception. Add this piece to a little boy's room decor for wall art that's sure to please! Design by Michele Wilcox

Skill Level
Beginner

Size
6⅛ inches W x 11 inches H (15.26cm x 27.9cm), excluding hanger

Materials
- 1 sheet 7-count plastic canvas
- Uniek Needloft plastic canvas yarn as listed in color key
- #3 pearl cotton as listed in color key
- #16 tapestry needle
- 22mm gold key ring
- Desired length ¼-inch/0.6cm-wide white satin ribbon for hanger

Instructions
1. Cut plastic canvas according to graph (page 85).

2. Stitch and Overcast piece following graph, working uncoded areas with white background in black Continental Stitches and uncoded areas with pale peach background in beige Continental Stitches.

3. When background stitching is completed, work pearl cotton embroidery.

4. Insert gold key ring in ear where indicated on graph. Attach ribbon through opening at top with a Lark's Head Knot. Tie ends together in a bow to form a loop for hanging. ✂

Graphs continued on page 85

Sleepy Moon Baby Decor

The gentle prayer of this darling wall hanging will guide baby into dreamland. Design by Mary Nell Wall

Skill Level

Beginner

Size

7½ inches W x 10¼ inches H (19.1cm x 26cm), including hanger

Materials

- ½ sheet 7-count clear plastic canvas
- ⅓ sheet 14-count white plastic canvas
- Coats & Clark Red Heart Classic worsted weight yarn Art. E267 as listed in color key
- #8 pearl cotton as listed in color key
- DMC 6-strand embroidery floss as listed in color key
- #16 tapestry needle
- 10 inches (25.4cm) ¼-inch/0.6cm-wide yellow grosgrain ribbon
- Sawtooth hanger
- Craft glue

Instructions

1. Following graphs (pages 80 and 81) throughout, cut moon and star from 7-count clear plastic canvas; cut cloud from 14-count white plastic canvas.

2. Stitch and Overcast moon and star following graphs. Work black and pink Backstitches on moon when stitching and Overcasting are completed.

3. Work Backstitches around cloud with 3 plies baby blue floss. Work lettering with pearl cotton. Do not Overcast.

4. Use photo as a guide through step 5. Insert ends of ribbon from back to front where indicated on moon graph, pulling ribbon all the way through. Glue ends together, then glue star over ends. Glue sawtooth hanger to back of star. Allow to dry.

5. Glue cloud to bottom left side of moon. Allow to dry. ✂

I see the Moon
and the Moon sees me
God bless the Moon
and God bless me!

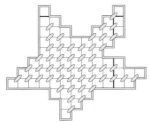

Sleepy Moon Star
13 holes x 11 holes
Cut 1 from 7-count clear

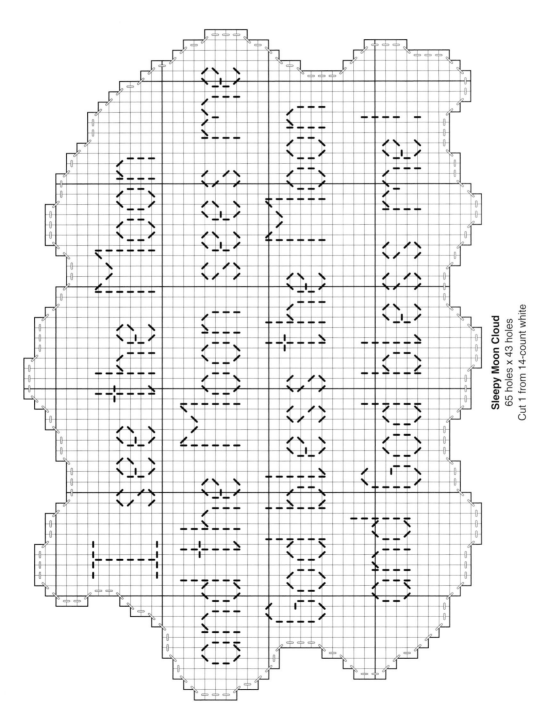

Sleepy Moon Cloud
65 holes x 43 holes
Cut 1 from 14-count white

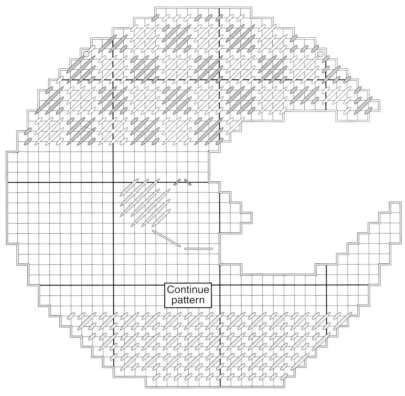

Sleepy Moon
37 holes x 37 holes
Cut 1 from 7-count clear

COLOR KEY		
Yards	**Worsted Weight Yarn**	
3 (2.8m)	☐ White #1	
8 (7.4m)	☐ Yellow #230	
1 (1m)	☐ Pink #737	
2 (1.9m)	▨ Light periwinkle #827	
1 (1m)	⟋ Black #12 Backstitch	
	⟋ Pink #737 Backstitch	
	#8 Pearl Cotton	
5 (4.6m)	✎ Black Backstitch and Straight Stitch	
	6-Strand Embroidery Floss	
3 (2.8m)	⟋ Baby blue #3755 (3-ply) Backstitch	
	○ Attach ribbon	

Color numbers given are for Coats & Clark Red Heart Classic worsted weight yarn Art. E267 and DMC 6-strand embroidery floss.

Beaded Bear Wind Chime

Hang this sweet bear close to a window so that the breeze blows through the ribbon and bead streamers. Design by Janelle Giese

Skill Level
Intermediate

Size
6 ⅛ inches W x 6 ⅞ inches H (15.6cm x 17/5cm), excluding streamers

Materials
• 1 sheet 7-count plastic canvas
• Coats & Clark Red Heart Classic worsted weight yarn Art. E267 as listed in color key
• #5 pearl cotton as listed in color key
• 1 yard (1m) red #321 6-strand embroidery floss
• #16 tapestry needle
• 5 each 6mm x 9mm heart pony bead: red, pink, white
• 3¼ yards (3m) ⅛-inch/0.3cm-wide red satin ribbon
• 2 yards (1.9m) ⅛-inch/0.3cm-wide ivory satin ribbon
• Hand-sewing needle
• Thick white glue

Cutting & Stitching
1. Cut plastic canvas according to graphs (page 84).

2. Cut red ribbon into five 18-inch (45.7cm) lengths for streamers and two 12-inch (30.5cm) lengths for hearts. Cut ivory ribbon into four 18-inch (45.7cm) lengths for streamers.

3. Following graphs throughout, stitch and Overcast hearts, working uncoded background with jockey red Continental Stitches. Stitch bears, working uncoded background with tan Continental Stitches.

4. Work French Knots for eyes of bears with black yarn, wrapping needle twice. Embroider features on bears with black pearl cotton; embroider lettering on hearts with white pearl cotton.

Assembly
1. Center each heart over one 12-inch (30.5cm) length of ribbon. Using hand-sewing needle and 2 plies red floss, tack in place at green dots.

2. Thread ribbon ends from front to back on bears where indicated with blue dots, then from back to front at red dots, pulling ribbon through on both sides so red heart is centered over heart on tummy. Tack ribbon in place on back side, using hand-sewing needle and 2 plies red floss. Trim ends as desired.

3. For hanger, thread ends of 13-inch (33cm) length of white pearl cotton through holes indicated with yellow dots at top of one bear; tie ends in a knot around top edge, so hanger is about 6 inches (15.2) long, trimming excess.

4. On each red streamer, tie a triple knot near one end and slide on a red bead. Tie a second knot about 1 inch (2.5cm) above the first knot and slide on a pink bead. Tie a third knot 1 inch (2.5cm) above second knot and slide on a white bead.

5. Place one bear face down on table. Glue streamers to back side, attaching red streamers at red arrows and ivory streamers at black arrows. Allow to dry. *Note: See photo for approximate lengths of streamers.* Trim excess ribbon above attachment points as needed.

6. Beginning at left foot and using a 1-yard (1m) length of warm brown, Whipstitch wrong sides of bears together across bottom edge, joining with Cross Stitches at streamers.

7. Continue Whipstitching all around bear with warm brown, working Cross Stitches where hanger is attached. ✄

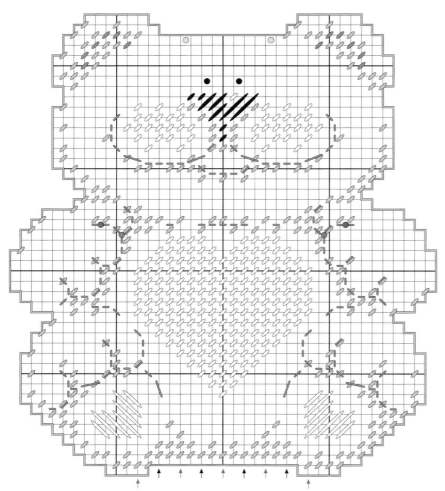

Beaded Bear
40 holes x 45 holes
Cut 2

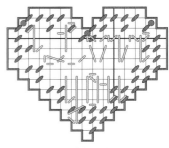

Beaded Bear Heart
15 holes x 13 holes
Cut 2

COLOR KEY	
Yards	**Worsted Weight Yarn**
1 (1m)	■ Black #12
9 (8.3m)	□ Eggshell #111
15 (13.8m)	▨ Warm brown #336
1 (1m)	▨ Mid brown #339
7 (6.5m)	▧ Cherry red #912
25 (22.9m)	Uncoded background on bear is tan #334 Continental Stitches
2 (1.9m)	Uncoded background on heart is jockey red #902 Continental Stitches
	● Black #12 French Knot
6 (5.5m)	**#5 Pearl Cotton**
3 (2.8m)	╱ Black Backstitch and Straight Stitch
	╱ White Backstitch
	● Tack ribbon to heart
	● Red ribbon entry point
	● Red ribbon exit point
	○ Attach hanger

Color numbers given are for Coats & Clark Red Heart Classic worsted weight yarn Art. #267.

Ahoy, Matey

Continued from page 77

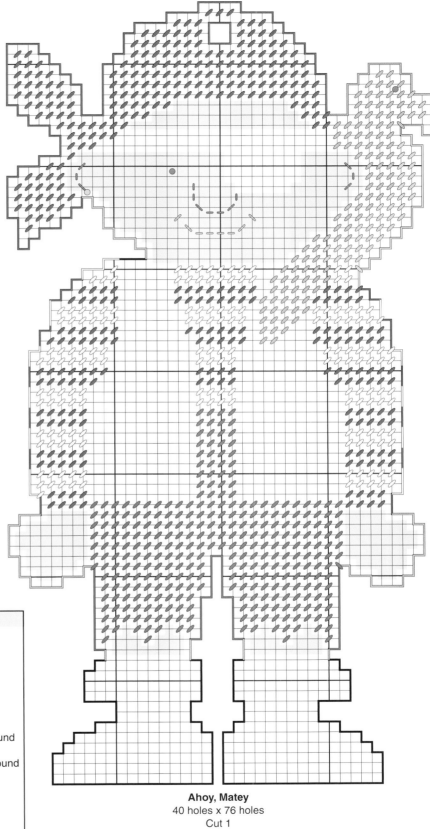

Ahoy, Matey
40 holes x 76 holes
Cut 1

COLOR KEY

Yards	Plastic Canvas Yarn
11 (11m)	■ Red #01
1 (1m)	☐ Tangerine #11
1 (1m)	■ Maple #13
3 (2.8m)	☐ Fern #23
8 (7.4m)	■ Royal #32
5 (4.6m)	☐ White #41
2 (1.9m)	☐ Yellow #57
16 (14.7m)	Uncoded areas with white background are black #00 Continental Stitches
10 (9.2m)	Uncoded areas with peach background are beige #40 Continental Stitches
	✐ Black #00 Overcasting
	⁄ Beige #40 Overcasting
	#3 Pearl Cotton
1 (1m)	⁄ Red Backstitch
1 (1m)	⁄ Black Backstitch
	● Black French Knot
	○ Attach gold key ring

Color numbers given are for Uniek Needloft plastic canvas yarn.

Darling Kitchen Decor

Step away from utilitarian kitchenware with sweet decor and accessory pieces. Bag clips, coasters and napkin rings are just a few of the cheerful designs to stitch.

Pigs in a Poke Coasters

These spunky pig coasters are in no hurry to go back to the barnyard—they're right at home in their mud-puddle holder.

Designs by Ronda Bryce

Skill Level
Beginner

Size
Pig Coaster: 5⅝ inches W x 5 inches H (14.3cm x 12.7cm)

Poke (Holder): 4⅝ inches W x 3⅞ inches H x 1⅝ inches D (11.7cm x 9.8cm x 4.1cm)

Materials
- 1 sheet clear 7-count plastic canvas
- 1 sheet brown 7-count plastic canvas
- Uniek Needloft plastic canvas yarn as listed in color key
- DMC 6-strand embroidery floss as listed in color key
- #16 tapestry needle
- 2 (¾-inch/1.9cm) pink ribbon flowers with leaves
- 2 (¾-inch/1.9cm) cream ribbon flowers with pearl centers
- Hand-sewing needle
- Pink and cream sewing thread

Instructions

1. Cut pig coasters from clear plastic canvas; cut poke pieces from brown plastic canvas according to graphs (pages 89, 90 and 91). Also cut one 30-hole x 10-hole piece from brown plastic canvas for poke base. Base will remain unstitched.

2. Stitch and Overcast pigs following graphs, working uncoded area on spotted pig with eggshell Continental Stitches and uncoded areas on saddleback pig with gray Continental Stitches.

3. When background stitching is completed, outline ear on white pig with very dark brown gray Backstitches.

4. Using sewing needle and pink sewing thread, attach pink ribbon flowers to white and pink pigs for tails.

5. Using sewing needle and cream sewing thread, attach cream ribbon flowers to spotted and saddleback pigs for tails.

6. Stitch holder front, back and sides following graphs. Using cinnamon throughout, Whipstitch front and back to sides, then Whipstitch front, back and sides to unstitched base; Overcast top edges. ✂

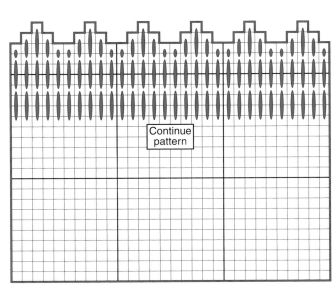

Poke Front & Back
30 holes x 25 holes
Cut 2 from brown

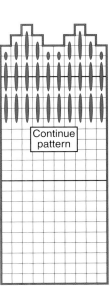

Poke Side
10 holes x 25 holes
Cut 2 from brown

COLOR KEY

Yards	Plastic Canvas Yarn
6 (5.5m)	■ Black #00
16 (14.7m)	□ Pink #07
30 (27.5m)	■ Cinnamon #14
11 (10.1m)	▦ Brown #15
14 (12.9m)	□ Eggshell #39
13 (11.9m)	□ White #41
5 (4.6m)	▨ Watermelon #55
11 (10.1m)	Uncoded areas on saddleback pig are gray #38 Continental Stitches
	Uncoded areas on spotted pig are eggshell #39 Continental Stitches

6-Strand Embroidery Floss

1 (1m)	╱ Very dark brown gray #3021 Backstitch
	● Attach pink flower
	○ Attach cream flower

Color numbers given are for Uniek Needloft plastic canvas yarn and DMC 6-strand embroidery floss.

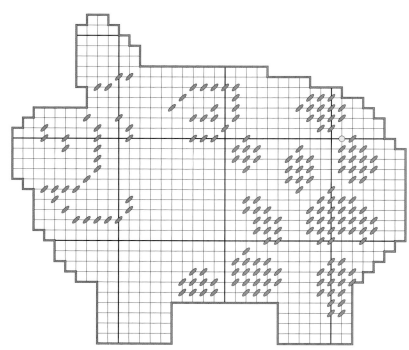

Spotted Pig Coaster
37 holes x 32 holes
Cut 1 from clear

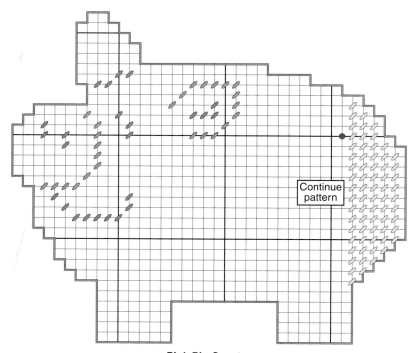

Pink Pig Coaster
37 holes x 32 holes
Cut 1 from clear

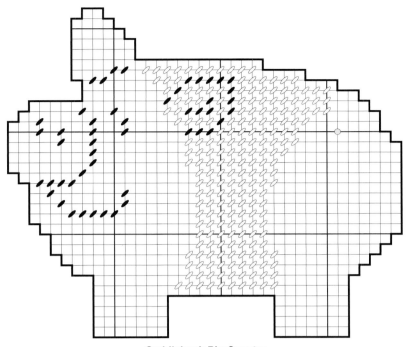

Saddleback Pig Coaster
37 holes x 32 holes
Cut 1 from clear

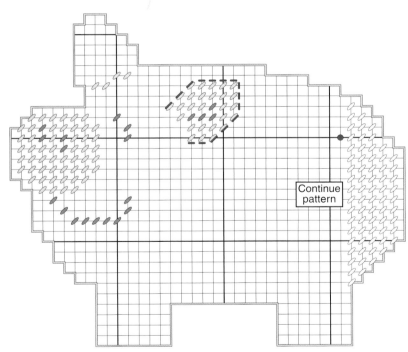

Continue
pattern

White Pig Coaster
37 holes x 32 holes
Cut 1 from clear

Santa Bear Coasters

Stitched on 10-count plastic canvas, these coasters feature bears dressed up as Santa and Mrs. Claus. Designs by Nancy Dorman

Skill Level
Beginner

Size
4 inches W x 4⅛ inches L (10.2cm x 10.5cm)

Materials
- 1 sheet 10-count plastic canvas
- Sport weight yarn as listed in color key
- ¹⁄₁₆-inch (2mm) Plastic Canvas 10 Metallic Needlepoint Yarn from Rainbow Gallery as listed in color key
- 6-strand embroidery floss as listed in color key
- #18 tapestry needle
- 4 (3¾-inch/9.5cm) squares ⅛-inch (0.3cm) cork
- Heavy books or weighted objects
- Craft glue

Instructions

1. Cut plastic canvas according to graphs (this page and pages 94 and 95)

2. Stitch and Overcast coasters following graphs, working uncoded backgrounds with dark blue Continental Stitches.

3. When background stitching and Overcasting are completed, work embroidery with metallic needlepoint yarn and floss. For garland on Christmas tree, first lay gold metallic needlepoint yarn, then couch same gold yarn where indicated.

4. For both green floss bows, lightly coat a 6-inch (15.2cm) length of 6-ply green floss with glue. Allow to dry, then tie in tiny bows. Glue to Mrs. Santa and Wreath coasters where indicated.

5. Glue cork to backs of coasters. Weight down with books or heavy objects until dry. ✄

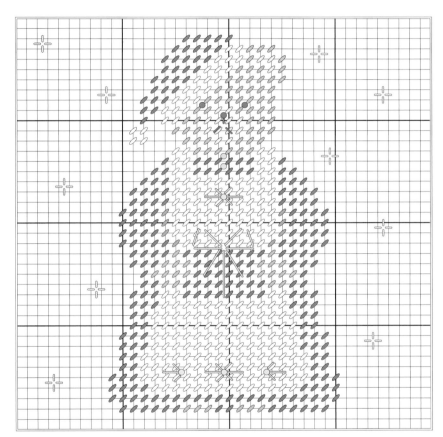

Mrs. Santa
39 holes x 40 holes
Cut 1

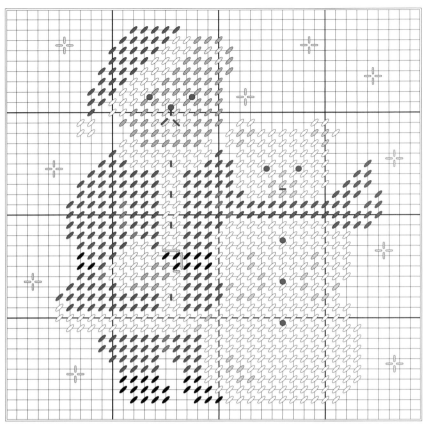

Santa & Polar Bear
39 holes x 40 holes
Cut 1

COLOR KEY	
Yards	**Sport Weight Yarn**
40 (36.6m)	☐ White
20 (18.3m)	■ Red
10 (9.2m)	■ Green
8 (7.4m)	▥ Medium brown
2 (1.9m)	☐ Tan
2 (1.9m)	■ Maroon
2 (1.9m)	☐ Light gray
2 (1.9m)	■ Black
50 (45.7m)	Uncoded backgrounds are dark blue Continental Stitches
	¹/₁₆-Inch (2mm) Metallic Needlepoint Yarn
3 (2.8m)	⟋ Gold #PM51 Backstitch, Straight Stitch and Laid Thread
	⟋ Gold #PM51 Couching Stitch
	○ Gold #PM51 French Knot
	6-Strand Embroidery Floss
4 (3.7m)	⟋ White Backstitch
2 (1.9m)	╱ Black Backstitch and Straight Stitch
2 (1.9m)	⟋ Green Backstitch
2 (1.9m)	○ Red French Knot
	● Black French Knot
	○ Attach green bow
Color number given is for Rainbow Gallery Plastic Canvas 10 Metallic Needlepoint Yarn.	

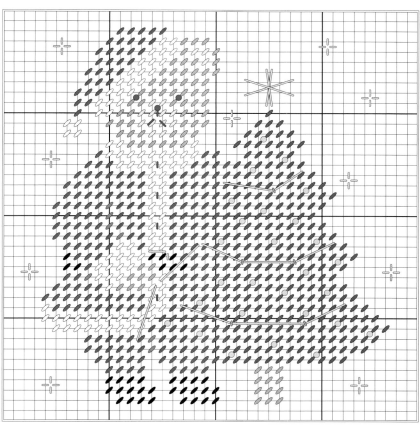

Santa & Christmas Tree
39 holes x 40 holes
Cut 1

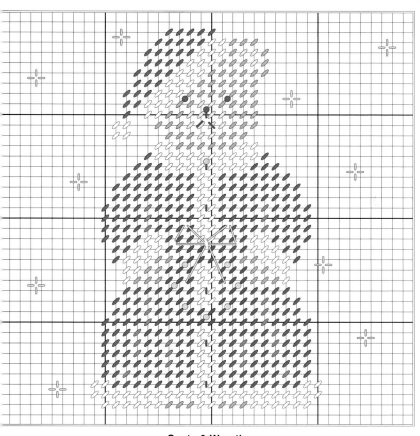

Santa & Wreath
39 holes x 40 holes
Cut 1

Apron Napkin Rings

Just right for informal dining, these little napkin rings are decorated with tiny flowers and buttons. Designs by Ronda Bryce

Skill Level
Beginner

Size
2¾ inches W x 3⅛ inches H (7cm x 8cm), excluding ties

Materials
Each
- Small amount 7-count plastic canvas
- Uniek Needloft plastic canvas yarn as listed in color key
- #16 tapestry needle
- 1 set Jesse James & Co. Inc. Dress It Up buttons: Sugar and Spice #TP-2460-4 (all but quilted apron)
- Hand-sewing needle

Daisy
- 1 yard (1m) ¹⁄₁₆-inch/3mm-wide white satin ribbon
- 7 inches (17.8cm) ¼-inch/6mm-wide yellow rickrack
- ½ inch (8mm) white daisy appliqué
- Sewing thread: white, yellow and fern

Embroidered
- DMC 6-strand embroidery floss as listed in color key
- 1 yard (1m) ¹⁄₁₆-inch/3mm-wide ivory satin ribbon
- ⁷⁄₁₆-inch (6mm) round red button
- ¼ yard (0.2m) ½-inch/8mm-wide ivory eyelet
- Sewing thread: red and ivory

Gingham
- 1 yard (1m) ¹⁄₁₆-inch/3mm-wide pink satin ribbon
- 2 (⁷⁄₁₆-inch/6mm) round pink buttons
- 6¼ inches (15.9cm) ½-inch/8mm-wide white lace
- Sewing thread: pink and white

Pink Flowers
- DMC 6-strand embroidery floss as listed in color key
- 1 yard (1m) ¹⁄₁₆-inch/3mm-wide pink satin ribbon
- 10 inches (25.4cm) ¼-inch/6mm-wide pink rickrack
- ½-inch (8mm) pink ribbon rose with leaves
- Sewing thread: pink and white

Quilted
- 1 yard (1m) ¹⁄₁₆-inch/3mm-wide white satin ribbon
- 5½ inches (14cm) ¼-inch/6mm-wide white lace
- ½-inch (8mm) blue ribbon rose with leaves
- Sewing thread: blue and white

Striped
- 1 yard (1m) ¹⁄₁₆-inch/3mm-wide red satin ribbon
- ¼-inch (7mm) red heart button
- Sewing thread: red and white

Cutting & Stitching

1. Cut aprons and pockets from plastic canvas according to graphs (pages 98 and 99).

2. Cut ¹⁄₁₆-inch/3mm-wide satin ribbon for each apron as follows: one 18-inch (45.7cm) length and two 6-inch (15.2cm) lengths.

3. Stitch and Overcast pieces following graphs, working uncoded backgrounds with white Continental Stitches.

4. When background stitching is completed, work red floss Backstitches and Running Stitches on embroidered apron and pockets. On pink flowers apron, work kelly green floss Backstitches and pink yarn French Knots.

5. Use hand-sewing needle and matching thread color through step 6. For waist ribbons, center and stitch 18-inch (45.7cm) lengths ribbon to yarn across backs of corresponding aprons where indicated with black arrows.

6. For neck ribbons, stitch ends of short lengths to backs of aprons where indicated with red arrows. For each apron, tie neck ribbons together in a knot about 1 inch (2.5cm) above top edge; trim ends as desired.

Daisy Apron

1. Cut yellow rickrack into one 4-inch (10.2cm) length and one 3-inch (7.6cm) length. Using hand-sewing needle and yellow thread, attach short length to bib of apron and long length to skirt of apron where indicated with yellow lines.

2. Using hand-sewing needle and white thread, stitch daisy appliqué to pocket front where indicated on graph.

3. Using hand-sewing needle and fern thread, stitch sides and bottom of pocket to apron front where indicated with gray shading.

4. Insert one rolling pin button in pocket.

Embroidered Apron

1. Using hand-sewing needle and ivory thread through step 2, stitch ivory eyelet to back of apron along bottom edge, turning ends under.

2. Sew sides and bottoms of pockets to apron front where indicated with gray shading. Insert handle of red spoon button in one pocket, then stitch shank to apron to secure.

3. Using hand-sewing needle and red thread, stitch round red button to bib of apron where indicated on graph.

Gingham Apron

1. Cut ½-inch/8mm-wide white lace into one 4-inch (10.2cm) length and two 1⅛-inch (2.9cm) lengths. Using hand-sewing needle and white thread, attach long length to front of apron along bottom edge, wrapping lace around to back of apron. Stitch one short length to back of each pocket along top edge.

2. Using hand-sewing needle and pink thread through step 3, stitch pink buttons to bib of apron where indicated on graph.

3. Stitch sides and bottoms of pockets to apron front where indicated with gray shading.

4. Insert cutting board button in one pocket and gingerbread man button in second pocket.

Pink Flowers Apron

1. Cut pink rickrack into two 4-inch (10.2cm) lengths and one 2-inch (5.1cm) length. Using hand-sewing needle and pink thread, attach short length to pocket and long lengths to skirt of apron where indicated with pink lines.

2. Using hand-sewing needle and pink thread, stitch pink ribbon rose to pocket front where indicated on graph.

3. Using hand-sewing needle and white thread, stitch sides and bottom of pocket to apron front where indicated with gray shading.

4. Insert gingerbread man button in pocket.

Quilted Apron

1. Cut ¼-inch/6mm-wide white lace into one 4-inch (10.2cm) length and one 1½-inch (3.8cm) length. Using hand-sewing needle and white thread, stitch short length to back of pocket along top edge, turnings ends under;

stitch long length to back of apron along bottom edge, turning ends under.

2. Using hand-sewing needle and blue thread, stitch blue ribbon rose to pocket front where indicated on graph.

Striped Apron

1. Using hand-sewing needle and red thread, stitch red heart button to bib of apron where indicated on graph.

2. Using hand-sewing needle and white thread, stitch sides and bottom of pocket to apron front where indicated with gray shading.

3. Insert rolling pin button in pocket.

Finishing

1. For each napkin ring, tie waist ribbons in a bow around napkin, pulling tight enough to curve apron. ✄

COLOR KEY	
Yards	**Plastic Canvas Yarn**
6 (5.5m)	■ Red #01
8 (7.4m)	□ Pink #07
4 (3.7m)	□ Fern #23
9 (8.3m)	□ Eggshell #39
21 (23m)	□ White #41
2 (1.9m)	□ Yellow #57
8 (7.4m)	□ Bright blue #60
	Uncoded backgrounds are white #41 Continental Stitches
	○ Pink #07 French Knot
	6-Strand Embroidery Floss
1 (1m)	╱ Red #321 Backstitch and Running Stitch
1 (1m)	╱ Kelly green #702 Backstitch
	○ Attach daisy
	● Attach round red button
	◉ Attach round pink button
	○ Attach ribbon rose
	♥ Attach red heart button
Color numbers given are for Uniek Needloft plastic canvas yarn and DMC 6-strand embroidery floss.	

Gingham Apron Pocket
7 holes x 7 holes
Cut 2

Quilted Apron Pocket
7 holes x 7 holes
Cut 1

Pink Flowers Apron Pocket
8 holes x 6 holes
Cut 1

Daisy Apron Pocket
7 holes x 6 holes
Cut 1

Embroidered Apron Pocket
7 holes x 7 holes
Cut 2

Striped Apron Pocket
6 holes x 5 holes
Cut 1

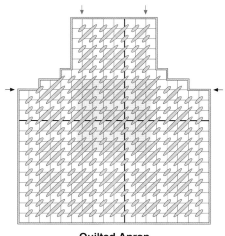

Quilted Apron
18 holes x 20 holes
Cut 1

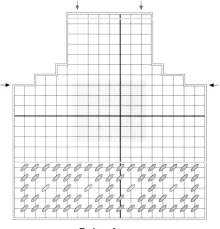

Daisy Apron
18 holes x 20 holes
Cut 1

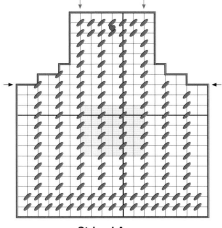

Striped Apron
18 holes x 20 holes
Cut 1

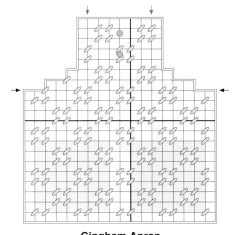

Gingham Apron
18 holes x 20 holes
Cut 1

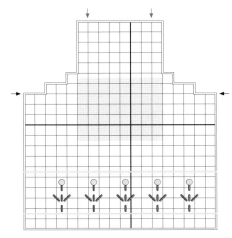

Pink Flowers Apron
18 holes x 20 holes
Cut 1

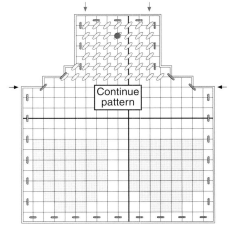

Continue
pattern

Embroidered Apron
18 holes x 20 holes
Cut 1

Summer Celebration Set

Get ready for a fun summer picnic with a checked napkin holder, and ladybug and dragonfly napkin rings. No ants allowed!

Designs by Michele Wilcox

Skill Level

Beginner

Size

Napkin Holder: 6⅞ inches W x 6½ inches H x 3¼ inches D (17.5cm x 16.5cm x 8.3cm), including handles

Dragonfly: 3⅞ inches W x 5 inches L (9.8cm x 12.7cm), excluding ring

Ladybug: 2⅝ inches W x 3⅛ inches L (6.7cm x 8cm), excluding ring

Materials

- 2 sheets 7-count plastic canvas
- Uniek Needloft plastic canvas yarn as listed in color key
- DMC #3 pearl cotton as listed in color key
- #16 tapestry needle
- 2 (4mm) black beads
- 2 (4mm) blue beads
- Hand-sewing needle
- Black sewing thread
- Hot-glue gun

Instructions

1. Cut plastic canvas according to graphs (pages 101 and 102).

2. Stitch and Overcast dragonfly, ladybug, doilies and handles following graphs, working uncoded area on dragonfly with fern Continental Stitches and uncoded background on ladybug with red Continental Stitches.

3. When background stitching and Overcasting are completed, work pearl cotton Backstitches and French Knots on doilies and black yarn Backstitches on ladybug.

4. Using sewing needle and black sewing thread, attach blue beads to ladybug and black beads to dragonfly for eyes.

5. Stitch napkin rings and holder front, back, sides and bottom, working dragonfly napkin ring with fern as graphed and ladybug ring with red.

6. For each napkin ring, using adjacent colors, Overcast long edges, then Whipstitch ends together. Glue seam side of rings to bugs where indicated on graphs with blue shading.

7. Using fern throughout, Whipstitch holder front and back to sides, then Whipstitch front, back and sides to bottom. Overcast top edges.

8. Glue doilies to front and back where indicated, making sure top edges are even. Fold one handle; glue wrong side of ends to one side where indicated on graph with pale peach shading. Glue remaining handle to other end. ✂

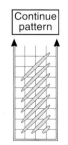

Holder Handle
4 holes x 46 holes
Cut 2

Continue
pattern

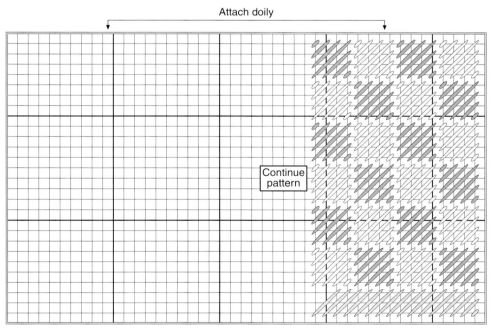

Attach doily

Continue
pattern

Holder Front & Back
45 holes x 28 holes
Cut 2

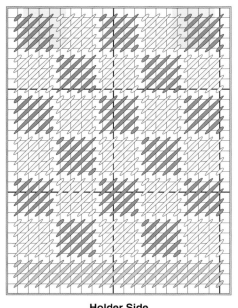

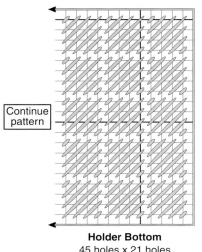

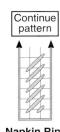

Holder Side
21 holes x 28 holes
Cut 2

Continue
pattern

Holder Bottom
45 holes x 21 holes
Cut 1

Continue
pattern

Napkin Ring
3 holes x 43 holes
Cut 2
Stitch 1 as graphed for dragonfly
Stitch 1 with red for ladybug

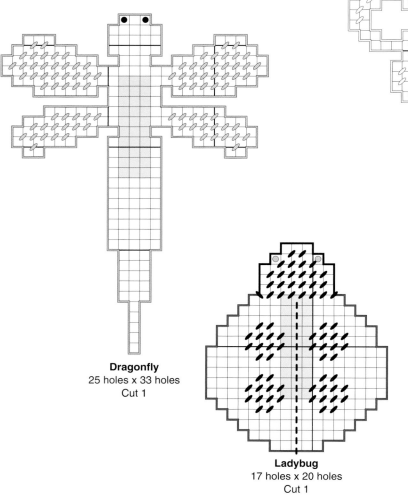

Dragonfly
25 holes x 33 holes
Cut 1

Ladybug
17 holes x 20 holes
Cut 1

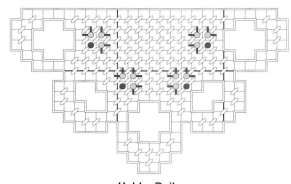

Holder Doily
26 holes x 16 holes
Cut 2

COLOR KEY	
Yards	**Plastic Canvas Yarn**
3 (2.8m)	■ Black #00
6 (5.5m)	▨ Tangerine #11
30 (27.5m)	▨ Pumpkin #12
30 (27.5m)	☐ Baby yellow #17
34 (31.1m)	▨ Fern #23
12 (11m)	☐ White #41
5 (4.6m)	Uncoded background on ladybug is red #01 Continental Stitches
	Uncoded area on dragonfly is fern #23 Continental Stitches
	╱ Back #00 Backstitch
	╱ Red #01 Overcasting
	#3 Pearl Cotton
2 (1.9m)	╱ Hunter green #3346 Backstitch
2 (1.9m)	◦ Burnt orange #947 French Knot
	● Hunter green #3346 French Knot
	◦ Attach blue bead
	● Attach black bead

Color numbers given are for Uniek Needloft plastic canvas yarn and DMC #3 pearl cotton.

Summertime Fridgies

You'll feel like you're at the beach, every time you see these fun flip-flop fridgies. Rhinestones, fluffy yarn and a silk flower add dimension. Designs by Nancy Dorman

Skill Level
Beginner

Size
1¾ inches W x 3¼ inches L (4.4cm x 8.3cm)

Materials
- ¼ sheet 7-count plastic canvas
- Worsted weight yarn as listed in color key
- #16 tapestry needle
- 4 inches (10.2cm) rhinestone trim
- 4 inches (10.2cm) green fluffy yarn of choice
- ⅞-inch (2.2cm) white silk flower
- 5 inches (12.7cm) magnet strip
- Hot-glue gun

Instructions
1. Cut plastic canvas according to graphs (page 119).

2. Stitch and Overcast flip-flops following graphs, working left flip-flop with yellow as graphed. Reverse two for right flip-flops; stitch one with turquoise and one with purple.

3. Stitch and Overcast one strap with lime green as graphed and one each with orange and bright pink.

4. Place flip-flops and straps together as follows: yellow flip-flop with lime green strap, turquoise flip-flop with orange strap, purple flip-flop with bright pink strap.

5. Using yarn color used for straps throughout, tack point of each strap to top of flip-flop where indicated on graph. Bend straps around to bottom of flip-flops and tack ends in place where indicated on graph.

6. Cut magnet strip into three lengths. Glue one length to bottom of each flip-flop.

7. To finish flip-flops, glue as follows: green fluffy yarn along top of lime green straps, rhinestone trim along top of bright pink straps and white silk flower to orange strap where indicated on graph. ✂

Graphs continued on page 119

Dairy Dudes Fridgie Friends

Nothing's more fun than a set of funky dairy characters!

Designs by Mary T. Cosgrove

Skill Level
Beginner

Size
Butter: 3⅜ inches W x 2 inches H (8.6cm x 5.1cm)
Cheese: 3⅜ inches W x 2⅝ inches H (8.6cm x 6.7cm)
Eggs: 3⅜ inches W x 2¼ inches H (8.6cm x 5.7cm)
Milk: 3⅜ inches W x 2½ inches H (8.6cm x 6.4cm)

Materials
• ½ sheet 7-count clear plastic canvas
• Uniek Needloft plastic canvas yarn as listed in color key

• #16 tapestry needle
• 4 (1-inch/2.5cm) lengths ½-inch/1.3cm-wide magnet strip
• Hot-glue gun

Instructions
1. Cut plastic canvas according to graphs.

2. Stitch and Overcast pieces following graphs, working uncoded backgrounds on butter and cheese with yellow Continental Stitches, uncoded background on eggs with gray Continental Stitches and uncoded background on milk with white Continental Stitches.

3. When background stitching and Overcasting are completed, use 1 ply yarn to work embroidery.

4. Glue one magnet strip to back of each piece. ✄

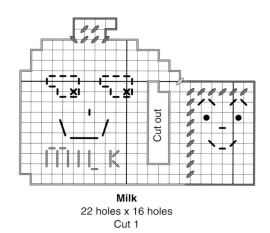

Milk
22 holes x 16 holes
Cut 1

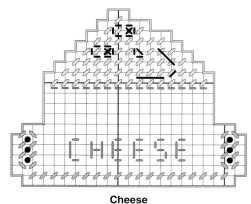

Cheese
22 holes x 17 holes
Cut 1

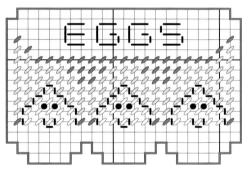

Eggs
22 holes x 15 holes
Cut 1

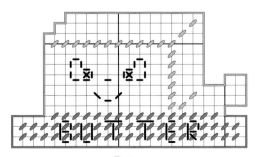

Butter
22 holes x 13 holes
Cut 1

COLOR KEY

Yards	Plastic Canvas Yarn
6 (5.5m)	■ Red #01
4 (3.7m)	☐ Tangerine #11
2 (1.9m)	☐ Pumpkin #12
4 (3.7m)	☐ Gray #38
5 (4.6m)	☐ White #41
	Uncoded background on eggs is gray #38 Continental Stitches
	Uncoded background on milk is white #41 Continental Stitches
5 (4.6m)	Uncoded backgrounds on butter and cheese are yellow #57 Continental Stitches
3 (2.8m)	╱ Black #00 (1-ply) Backstitch, Straight Stitch and Cross Stitch
	╱ Red #01 (1-ply) Backstitch and Straight Stitch
	╱ Yellow #57 Overcasting
	● Black #00 (1-ply) French Knot

Color numbers given are for Uniek Needloft plastic canvas yarn.

Happy Hound Towel Holder

Forget about playing fetch—this friendly pup will always keep your towel close at hand. Design by Debbie Tabor

Skill Level

Beginner

Size

9¾ inches W x 9¼ inches H (24.8cm x 23.5cm), excluding ribbon hanger

Materials

- 2 sheets 7-count plastic canvas
- Coats & Clark Red Heart Classic worsted weight yarn Art. E267 as listed in color key
- #16 tapestry needle
- 12 inches (30.5cm) 1-inch/2.5cm-wide pink satin ribbon (or color to match decor)
- Small amount 6-strand embroidery floss in color to match ribbon

Instructions

1. Cut front and back from plastic canvas according to graph (page 113). Back piece will remain unstitched.

2. Stitch front following graph, working uncoded background with white Continental Stitches.

3. When background stitching is completed, work black Backstitches and white French Knots, wrapping yarn three times.

4. Fold ribbon in half and place ends on unstitched back where indicated on graph with blue highlighting. Use floss to stitch to canvas 5 holes from top.

5. Overcast top edges of front from arrow to arrow. With ribbon between pieces, Whipstitch front and back together along inside edges and remaining outside edges.

6. Insert hand towel through opening for tongue. ✄

Graphs continued on page 113

Precious Pets' Food Clips

Add a sweet touch to a bag of pet food by keeping it closed with a special clip. Designs by Janelle Giese

Skill Level
Intermediate

Size
Kitty Food: 7⅛ inches W x 5½ inches H (18.1cm x 14cm)
Doggy Food: 7⅜ inches W x 6 inches H (18.7cm x 15.2cm)
Birdie Seed: 7⅜ inches W x 5⅝ inches H (18.7cm x 14.3cm), excluding tuft

Materials
Each Motif
- ½ sheet 7-count plastic canvas
- Uniek Needloft plastic canvas yarn as listed in color key
- #3 pearl cotton as listed in color key
- #5 pearl cotton as listed in color key
- #16 tapestry needle
- 6-inch-wide x 3¼-inch-high (15.2cm x 8.3cm) purchased bag clip
- Carpet thread
- Thick white glue

Kitty Food
1. Cut plastic canvas according to graph (page 110).

2. Stitch and Overcast piece following graph, working uncoded background on kitty with silver Continental Stitches and uncoded background on sign with baby yellow Continental Stitches.

3. When background stitching and Overcasting are completed, use full strands yarn to work pink Straight Stitch for slash on sign and moss Straight Stitches for eye color.

4. Embroider lettering and Backstitches around pink slash on sign with black #3 pearl cotton, wrapping needle twice for French Knot. Use black #5 pearl cotton to embroider kitty features.

5. Using 1 ply white, work eye highlights.

6. Center and glue stitched piece over clip so that bottom of clip is about two bars above bottom edge of sign. Use carpet thread to sew ends of clip front to yarn on back of stitched piece.

Doggy Food
1. Cut plastic canvas according to graph (page 111).

2. Stitch and Overcast piece following graph, working uncoded background on doggy with beige Continental Stitches and uncoded background on sign with white Continental Stitches.

3. When background stitching and Overcasting are completed, use full strands yarn to work red Straight Stitch for slash on sign and cinnamon Straight Stitches for eye color.

4. Embroider lettering and Backstitches around red slash on sign with black #3 pearl cotton. Use black #5 pearl cotton to embroider doggy features, wrapping needle twice for French Knots.

5. Using 1 ply white, work eye highlights.

6. Center and glue stitched piece over clip so that bottom of clip is about one bar above bottom edge of sign. Use carpet thread to sew ends of clip front to yarn on back of stitched piece.

Birdie Seed

1. Cut plastic canvas according to graph (page 112).

2. Stitch and Overcast piece following graph, working uncoded background on birdie with white Continental Stitches and uncoded background on sign with eggshell Continental Stitches.

3. When background stitching and Overcasting are completed, use full strands yarn to work yellow Straight Stitches for slash on sign, for eye color and center of beak; work Straight Stitches on wings with white.

4. Embroider lettering and Backstitches around yellow slash on sign with black #3 pearl cotton, wrapping needle twice for French Knots. Use black #5 pearl cotton to embroider birdie features.

5. Using 1 ply white, work eye highlights. For tuft, place one length each of baby blue and white together and attach to top of head where indicated with a Lark's Head Knot. Trim to ¾ inch (1.9cm) and fray.

6. Center and glue stitched piece over clip so that bottom of clip is about one bar above bottom edge of sign. Use carpet thread to sew ends of clip front to yarn on back of stitched piece. ✄

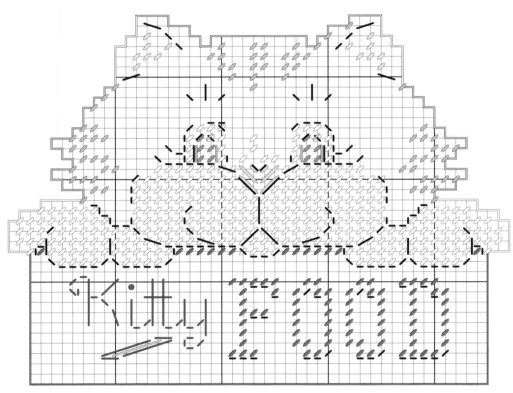

Kitty Food
47 holes x 36 holes
Cut 1

COLOR KEY		
KITTY FOOD		
Yards	**Plastic Canvas Yarn**	
1 (1m)	■ Black #00	
4 (3.7m)	■ Red #01	
1 (1m)	□ Pink #07	
3 (2.8m)	▨ Gray #38	
6 (5.5m)	□ White #41	
7 (6.5m)	Uncoded background on sign is baby yellow #21 Continental Stitches	
6 (5.5m)	Uncoded background on kitty is silver #37 Continental Stitches	
	⁄ Pink #07 (2-ply) Straight Stitch	
1 (1m)	⁄ Moss #25 (2-ply) Straight Stitch	
	⁄ Silver #37 Overcasting	
	⁄ White #41 (1-ply) Straight Stitch	
1 (1m)	**#3 Pearl Cotton**	
	╱ Black Backstitch and Straight Stitch	
	● Black (2-wrap) French Knot	
5 (4.6m)	**#5 Pearl Cotton**	
	╱ Black Backstitch and Straight Stitch	
Color numbers given are for Uniek Needloft plastic canvas yarn.		

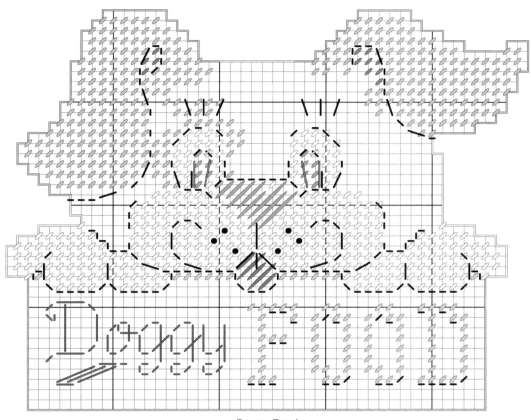

Doggy Food
49 holes x 39 holes
Cut 1

COLOR KEY
DOGGY FOOD

Yards	Plastic Canvas Yarn
1 (1m)	■ Black #00
1 (1m)	■ Red #01
1 (1m)	■ Cinnamon #14
5 (4.6m)	□ Eggshell #39
8 (7.4m)	□ White #41
7 (6.5m)	■ Camel #43
3 (2.8m)	■ Bittersweet #52
5 (4.6m)	Uncoded background on doggy is beige #40 Continental Stitches
	Uncoded background on sign is white #41 Continental Stitches
	╱ Red #01 (2-ply) Straight Stitch
	╱ Cinnamon #14 (2-ply) Straight Stitch
	╱ Beige #40 Overcasting
	╱ White #41 (1-ply) Straight Stitch

#3 Pearl Cotton

2 (1.9m)	╱ Black Backstitch and Straight Stitch

#5 Pearl Cotton

5 (4.6m)	╱ Black Backstitch and Straight Stitch
	● Black (2-wrap) French Knot

Color numbers given are for Uniek Needloft plastic canvas yarn.

Birdie Seed
49 holes x 37 holes
Cut 1

COLOR KEY		
BIRDIE SEED		
Yards	**Plastic Canvas Yarn**	
1 (1m)	■	Black #00
7 (6.5m)	□	Baby blue #36
3 (2.8m)	▨	Watermelon #55
1 (1m)	□	Yellow #57
7 (6.5m)		Uncoded background on sign is eggshell #39 Continental Stitches
7 (6.5m)		Uncoded background on birdie is white #41 Continental Stitches
	⁄	White #41 (2-ply) Straight Stitch
	⁄	White #41 (1-ply) Straight Stitch
	⁄	Yellow #57 (2-ply) Straight Stitch
	○	Baby blue #36 and white #41 Lark's Head Knot
	#3 Pearl Cotton	
1 (1m)	⁄	Black Backstitch and Straight Stitch
	●	Black (2-wrap) French Knot
	#5 Pearl Cotton	
4 (3.7m)	⁄	Black Backstitch and Straight Stitch
Color numbers given are for Uniek Needloft plastic canvas yarn.		

Happy Hound Towel Holder

Continued from page 107

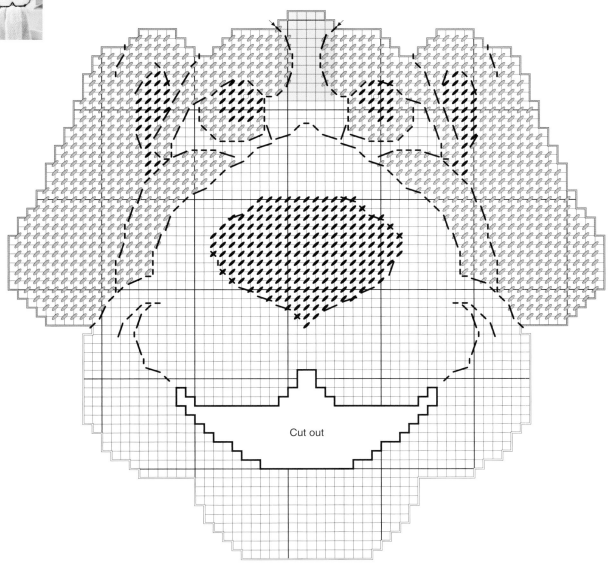

Happy Hound Holder Front & Back
64 holes x 61 holes
Cut 2
Stitch front only

Cut out

COLOR KEY	
Yards	**Worsted Weight Yarn**
12 (11m)	■ Black #12
18 (16.5m)	▨ Mid brown #339
12 (11m)	Uncoded background is white
4 (3.7m)	#1 Continental Stitches
	⁄ White #1 Whipstitching
	╱ Black #12 Backstitch
	○ White #1 (3-wrap) French Knot
Color numbers given are for Coats & Clark Red Heart Classic worsted weight yarn Art. E267.	

Couch Potato Bag Clip

Snack away—your chips will stay fresh when sealed with a clip decorated with a cozy little couch potato! Design by Janelle Giese

Skill Level
Intermediate

Size
7¼ inches W x 5¼ inches H (18.4cm x 13.3cm)

Materials
- ½ sheet 7-count plastic canvas
- Uniek Needloft plastic canvas yarn as listed in color key
- DMC #3 pearl cotton as listed in color key
- #5 pearl cotton as listed in color key
- #16 tapestry needle
- 6-inch-wide x 3¼-inch-high (15.2cm x 8.3cm) purchased bag clip
- Carpet thread
- Thick white glue

Instructions

1. Cut plastic canvas according to graph.

2. Stitch and Overcast piece following graph, working uncoded areas on white background with beige Continental Stitches and uncoded areas on pale yellow background with yellow Continental Stitches.

3. When background stitching and Overcasting are completed, use a full strand black yarn to work two Straight Stitches over center of each eye as indicated. Using 1 ply white, work eye highlights, coming up at top corner of each eye and down between black Straight Stitches.

4. Using black #5 pearl cotton, work embroidery, passing over eyelids twice. Using bright red #3 pearl cotton, embroider "POTATO CHIPS" and work French Knot for hat button, wrapping needle twice.

5. Center and glue stitched piece over clip so that bottom of clip is about one bar above bottom edge. Use carpet thread to sew ends of clip front to yarn on back of stitched piece. ✄

COLOR KEY		
Yards	**Plastic Canvas Yarn**	
1 (1m)	■ Black #00	
3 (2.8m)	■ Christmas red #02	
2 (1.9m)	▨ Fern #23	
2 (1.9m)	■ Royal #32	
4 (3.7m)	☐ White #41	
2 (1.9m)	▨ Camel #43	
6 (5.6m)	☐ Yellow #57	
3 (2.8m)	Uncoded areas on white background are beige #40 Continental Stitches	
	Uncoded area on pale yellow background is yellow #57 Continental Stitches	
	✎ Black #00 (2-ply) Straight Stitch	
	✎ White #41 (1-ply) Straight Stitch	
	#3 Pearl Cotton	
1 (1m)	✎ Bright red #666 Backstitch and Straight Stitch	
	○ Bright red #666 (2-wrap) French Knot	
	#5 Pearl Cotton	
5 (4.6m)	✎ Black Backstitch and Straight Stitch	

Color numbers given are for Uniek Needloft plastic canvas yarn and DMC #3 pearl cotton.

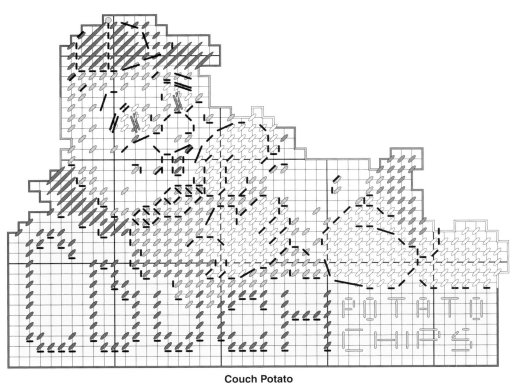

Couch Potato
47 holes x 34 holes
Cut 1

Calico Kitty Note Clip

This watchful kitty won't let your important notes out of her paws.

Design by Deborah Scheblein

Skill Level
Beginner

Size
5⅛ inches W x 5¾ inches H (13cm x 14.6cm)

Materials
- ½ sheet 7-count clear plastic canvas
- Worsted weight yarn as listed in color key
- #16 tapestry needle
- 1⅞-inch (4.8cm) spring clothespin
- 2 (12mm) green cat eyes
- 12mm animal "D" nose
- Button shank remover
- Hot-glue gun

Instructions
1. Cut plastic canvas according to graphs.

2. Stitch and Overcast head and body following graphs, placing tail support behind tail on body before stitching and working uncoded areas with white Continental Stitches.

3. When background stitching and Overcasting are completed, work Backstitches on paws with black and white and Straight Stitches on ears with pink.

4. Glue clothespin to center bottom of body front where indicated with arrow. Glue cat head to front of clothespin at a slight angle. Cut shanks from eyes and nose, then glue to head where indicated on graph.

5. Hang tail over cabinet knob or handle. ✂

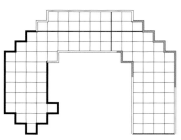

Calico Kitty Tail Support
16 holes x 12 holes
Cut 1
Place behind tail
on kitty body

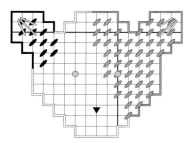

Calico Kitty Head
16 holes x 12 holes
Cut 1

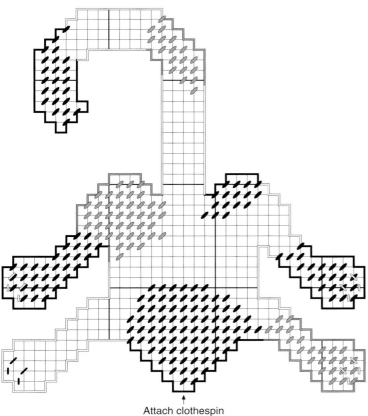

Attach clothespin

Calico Kitty Body
34 holes x 37 holes
Cut 1

COLOR KEY

Yards	Worsted Weight Yarn
5 (4.6m)	■ Black
4 (3.7m)	■ Rust
6 (5.5m)	Uncoded areas are white Continental Stitches
	⁄ White Backstitch and Overcasting
	⁄ Black Backstitch
1 (1m)	⁄ Pink Straight Stitch
	● Attach eye
	▼ Attach nose

Floral Trellis Photo Holder

Twisted wire on this trellis holder mimics the look of twining vines that hold treasured photos. Stitched flowers and leaves add the finishing touch. Design by Terry Ricioli

Skill Level
Beginner

Size
9 inches W x 13¾ inches H (22.9cm x 34.9cm), excluding coiled wire

Materials
- 1 sheet 7-count plastic canvas
- Uniek Needloft plastic canvas yarn as listed in color key
- #16 tapestry needle
- 6 (18-inch/45.7cm) lengths 20-gauge green craft wire
- Round-nose pliers
- Wire cutters
- Hot-glue gun

Instructions
1. Cut plastic canvas according to graphs.

2. Stitch and Overcast pieces following graphs.

3. Using photo as a guide and following Fig. 1 through step 4, glue uprights and crossbars together. Glue on flowers and leaves.

4. To wrap wire around trellis, glue one end of each length to back side, then wrap around trellis as desired. Coil remaining ends in a swirl, using round-nose pliers to begin and continuing with fingers and pliers as needed. Use wire cutters to trim wires to desired length. Glue wire on back of stitched pieces as needed to stabilize.

5. Hang trellis from crossbar or add hanger to back. Slide photos into swirls. ✂

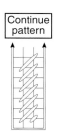

Continue pattern

Trellis Upright
3 holes x 90 holes
Cut 3

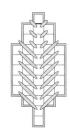

Trellis Leaf
5 holes x 11 holes
Cut 10

Continue pattern

Trellis Crossbar
49 holes x 3 holes
Cut 1
36 holes x 3 holes
Cut 1
25 holes x 3 holes
Cut 1

Trellis Flower
7 holes x 7 holes
Cut 9

COLOR KEY	
Yards	**Plastic Canvas Yarn**
10 (9.2m)	☐ Fern #23
25 (22.9m)	☐ White #41
12 (11m)	■ Watermelon #55
4 (3.7m)	☐ Yellow #57
Color numbers given are for Uniek Needloft plastic canvas yarn.	

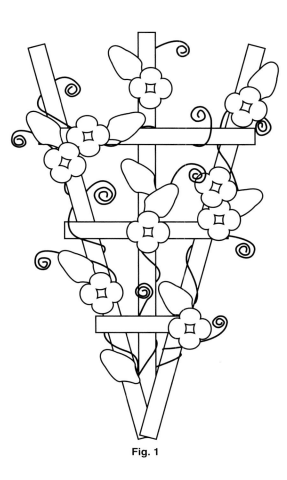

Fig. 1

Summertime Fridges

Continued from page 103

COLOR KEY	
Yards	**Worsted Weight Yarn**
5 (4.6m)	☐ Yellow
5 (4.6m)	Turquoise
5 (4.6m)	Purple
2 (1.9m)	╱ Lime green Overcasting
2 (1.9m)	Orange Overcasting
2 (1.9m)	Bright pink Overcasting
	● Attach strap point
	● Attach strap end
	○ Attach silk flower

Tack point to flip-flop

Flip-Flop Strap
17 holes x 17 holes
Cut 3
Stitch 1 as graphed
and 1 each with orange
and bright pink

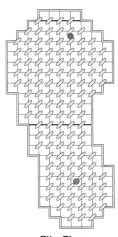

Flip-Flop
10 holes x 21 holes
Cut 3
Stitch 1 as graphed for left flip-flop
Reverse 2 for right flip-flops
Stitch 1 with turquoise
and 1 with purple

Floral Fantasy Frames

Nothing could make a flower prettier than adding a cherished photo of your family or friends to the center. Designs by Nancy Knapp

Skill Level
Intermediate

Size
Daisy: 8 inches W x 7¾ inches H x 3⅝ inches D (20.3cm x 19.7cm x 9.2cm); photo opening is 2⅜ inches (6cm) in diameter

Sunflower: 8½ inches W x 8 inches H x 3⅜ inches D (21.6cm x 20.3cm x 8.6cm); photo opening is 2⅜ inches (6cm) in diameter

Rose: 7¾ inches W x 7 inches H x 3⅜ inches D (19.7cm x 17.8cm x 8.6cm); photo opening is 2⅜ inches (6cm) in diameter

Materials
Each Frame
- Worsted weight yarn as listed in color key
- #16 tapestry needle
- 4½-inch (11.4cm) plastic canvas radial circle

Daisy Frame
- 4 sheets 7-count plastic canvas

Sunflower Frame
- 4 sheets 7-count plastic canvas

Rose Frame
- ¼ sheet 7-count plastic canvas
- 10 (3-inch/7.6cm) plastic canvas radial circles
- 2 (6-inch/15.2cm) plastic canvas radial circles

Daisy Frame Cutting & Stitching
1. Cut four flower sections, two supports and two braces from plastic canvas according to graphs (pages 122 and 125).

2. Cut frame center from 4½-inch (11.4cm) plastic canvas radial circle (page 123), cutting away gray areas.

3. Following graphs throughout, stitch flower sections. Stitch support and brace pieces with white. Using light gold, stitch flower center; Overcast inside and outside edges. Do not work running stitches at this time.

Daisy Frame Assembly
1. Using white through step 3, Whipstitch wrong sides of brace pieces together along side edges, then Whipstitch bottom edges of assembled brace to right side of one support piece where indicated with red highlighted line.

2. Whipstitch wrong sides of support pieces together around side and bottom edges.

3. Whipstitch top edges of assembled support to right side of one flower section at green highlighted line; Whipstitch bottom brace edges to flower section at blue highlighted line.

4. Whipstitch wrong sides of two flower sections together; repeat with remaining flower sections.

5. Use photo as a guide through step 8. Placing section with support in back, layer flower sections together so that petals on top piece are between petals of bottom piece.

6. With right side facing up, position frame center on top over middle of flower; work light gold running stitches around perimeter of circle, stitching along bottom half only and working through all layers.

7. When frame center is attached along bottom half, continue stitching flower sections together around perimeter of light gold stitching on flower sections to hold two sections together.

8. Trim photo to fit, then insert behind flower center.

Sunflower Frame

1. Cut four flower sections, two supports and two braces from plastic canvas according to graphs (this page and page 124).

2. Cut frame center from 4½-inch (11.4cm) plastic canvas radial circle (page 123), cutting away gray areas.

3. Following graphs throughout, stitch flower sections. Stitch support and brace pieces with gold. Using brown, stitch flower center; Overcast inside and outside edges.

4. Following assembly instructions for daisy frame, construct sunflower, using gold for support and brace, and brown for attaching frame center.

Rose Frame Cutting & Stitching

1. Cut two supports and two braces from plastic canvas according to graphs.

2. Cut frame center from 4½-inch (11.4cm) plastic canvas radial circle and 10 rose petals from 3-inch

(7.6cm) plastic canvas radial circles (this page and page 123), cutting away gray areas.

3. Following graphs and using rose yarn throughout, stitch base pieces (page 123), supports and braces. Stitch flower center; Overcast inside and outside edges. Do not work Backstitches at this time.

4. Stitch each rose petal, working Backstitches when background stitching is completed; Overcast curved edge.

Rose Frame Assembly

1. Use rose yarn throughout assembly. Following steps 1–3 for daisy frame assembly, put together brace and support pieces, attaching to right side of one base piece.

2. Use photo as a guide through step 5. With right side facing up, center frame center on right side of remaining base (base front); work Backstitches around perimeter of circle, stitching along bottom half only and working through both layers.

3. Evenly space five petals around base front; tack in place. Place remaining five petals behind and between first five petals; tack in place.

4. Whipstitch wrong sides of base pieces together around outer edge of base itself, working through all layers.

5. Trim photo to fit, then insert behind flower center. ✄

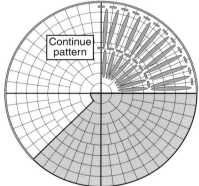

Rose Frame Petal
Cut 10 from
3-inch (7.6cm) radial circles,
cutting away gray area

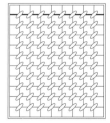

Frame Brace
9 holes x 11 holes
Cut 2 for each frame
Stitch as graphed for daisy frame
Stitch with gold for sunflower frame
Stitch with rose for rose frame

Frame Support
9 holes x 31 holes
Cut 2 for each frame
Stitch as graphed for daisy frame
Stitch with gold for sunflower frame
Stitch with rose for rose frame

COLOR KEY

Yards	Worsted Weight Yarn
80 (73.2m)	▨ Rose
60 (54.9m)	▨ Gold
42 (38.4m)	☐ White
40 (38.4m)	▨ Brown
36 (33m)	☐ Light gold
	✎ Rose Backstitch
	✎ Brown Running Stitch
	✎ Light gold Running Stitch

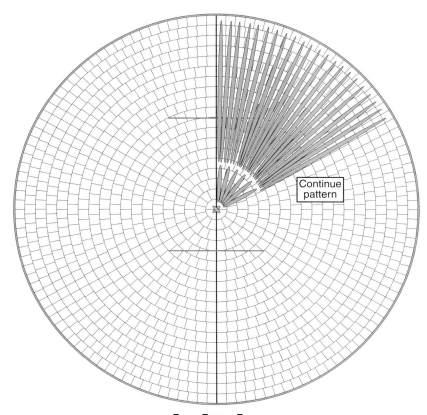

Rose Frame Base
Stitch 2 (6-inch/15.2cm) radial circles

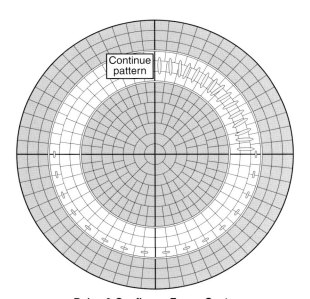

Daisy & Sunflower Frame Center
Cut 1 for each from
4½-inch (11.4cm) radial circle,
cutting away gray areas
Stitch as graphed for daisy frame
Stitch with brown for sunflower frame

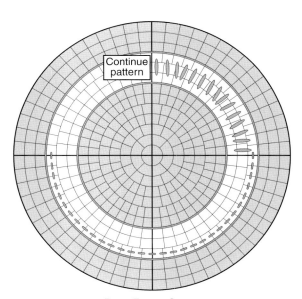

Rose Frame Center
Cut 1 from 4½-inch (11.4cm)
radial circle, cutting
away gray areas

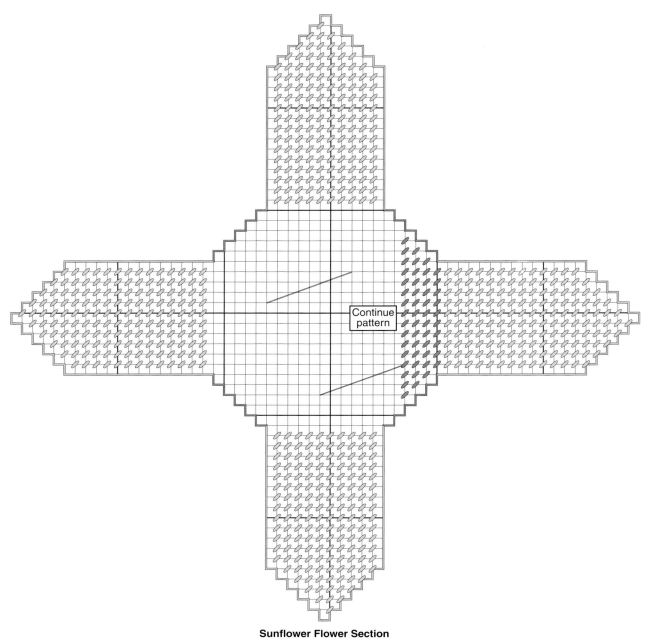

Continue
pattern

Sunflower Flower Section
59 holes x 59 holes
Cut 4

COLOR KEY	
Yards	**Worsted Weight Yarn**
80 (73.2m)	■ Rose
60 (54.9m)	■ Gold
42 (38.4m)	□ White
40 (38.4m)	■ Brown
36 (33m)	□ Light gold
	╱ Rose Backstitch
	╱ Brown Running Stitch
	╱ Light gold Running Stitch

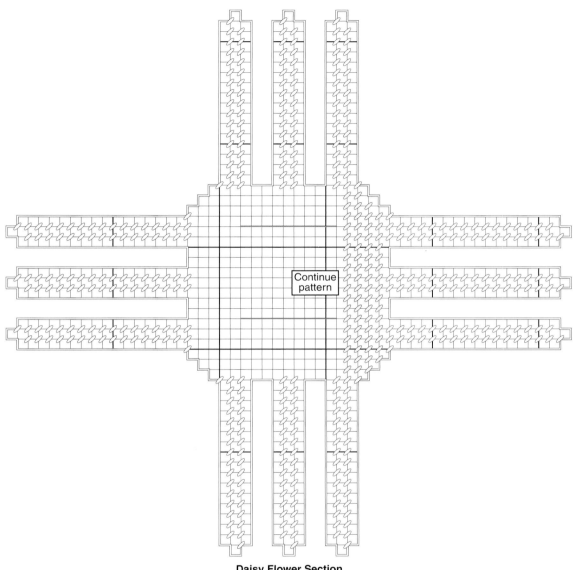

Daisy Flower Section
53 holes x 53 holes
Cut 4

Continue pattern

COLOR KEY	
Yards	**Worsted Weight Yarn**
80 (73.2m)	▨ Rose
60 (54.9m)	▨ Gold
42 (38.4m)	☐ White
40 (38.4m)	■ Brown
36 (33m)	☐ Light gold
	✎ Rose Backstitch
	✎ Brown Running Stitch
	✎ Light gold Running Stitch

Plant Poke Buddies

Add a whimsical touch to your favorite potted plants with a fun plant poke. Designs by Kathleen Hurley

Skill Level
Beginner

Size
Bee: 5 inches W x 2⅛ inches H (12.7cm x 5.4cm), excluding poke

Frog: 4 inches W x 4 inches H (10.2cm x 10.2cm), excluding poke

Ladybug With Legs & Antennae: 4¼ inches W x 3½ inches H (12.7cm x 8.9cm), excluding poke

Materials
- ½ sheet 7-count plastic canvas
- Coats & Clark Red Heart Classic worsted weight yarn Art. E267 as listed in color key
- #16 tapestry needle
- 1 yard (1m) ⅛-inch/0.3cm dowel
- 14 inches (35.6cm) 24-gauge black wire
- Hot-glue gun

Instructions

1. Cut plastic canvas according to graphs.

2. Stitch and Overcast pieces following graphs, working uncoded area on frog with emerald green Continental Stitches.

3. When background stitching and Overcasting are completed, work Backstitches and Straight Stitches on frog and ladybug with 2 plies black yarn.

4. Using photo as a guide through step 6, cut seven

2-inch (5.1cm) lengths of black wire. For legs, bend six lengths in half at right angles to form knees, then bend ⅛ inch (0.3cm) of one end on each to form feet. Glue wires to back of ladybug body at arrows.

5. Bend remaining wire in a "V" and fold down ⅛ inch (0.3cm) on each end. Center and glue to back of head for antennae.

6. Cut dowel in three pieces, varying lengths slightly. Glue one length to back of each buddy. ✄

Frog Buddy
26 holes x 26 holes
Cut 1

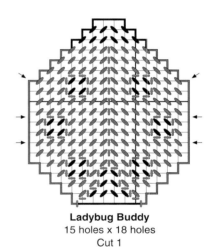

Ladybug Buddy
15 holes x 18 holes
Cut 1

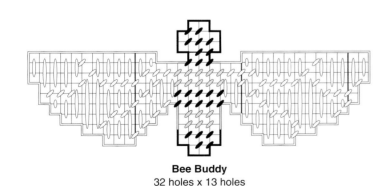

Bee Buddy
32 holes x 13 holes
Cut 1

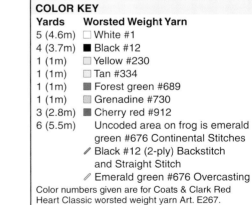

COLOR KEY	
Yards	**Worsted Weight Yarn**
5 (4.6m)	☐ White #1
4 (3.7m)	■ Black #12
1 (1m)	☐ Yellow #230
1 (1m)	☐ Tan #334
1 (1m)	■ Forest green #689
1 (1m)	☐ Grenadine #730
3 (2.8m)	■ Cherry red #912
6 (5.5m)	Uncoded area on frog is emerald green #676 Continental Stitches
	✎ Black #12 (2-ply) Backstitch and Straight Stitch
	✎ Emerald green #676 Overcasting

Color numbers given are for Coats & Clark Red Heart Classic worsted weight yarn Art. E267.

Sweet Sit-Arounds

Nothing starts a conversation quicker than adorable sit-arounds. Place these cute projects on a shelf, entryway table or buffet for you and your guests to enjoy!

Bluebird Songs

Cheer up your home and conceal your treasures in this birdhouse box featuring a realistic pedestal base. Design by Janelle Giese

Skill Level
Advanced

Size
5½ inches W x 9¼ inches H x 5⅜ inches D
(14cm x 23.5cm x 13.7cm)

Materials
- 2½ sheets 7-count plastic canvas
- Coats & Clark Red Heart Classic worsted weight yarn Art. E267 as listed in color key
- #5 pearl cotton as listed in color key
- #16 tapestry needle
- Small amount off-white felt
- 1½ cups aquarium gravel
- Thick white glue

Cutting & Stitching
1. Cut plastic canvas according to graphs (pages 131, 132 and 133), cutting out inside edges on bluebird and house front. *Note: Do not use red lines on birdhouse front, back and sides for cutting lines.*

2. Cut one 27-hole x 27 hole piece for pedestal base bottom, which will remain unstitched. Cut off-white felt slightly smaller all around than base bottom. Set aside.

3. Stitch and Overcast bluebird following graph, working uncoded background with eggshell Continental Stitches. Stitch leaves with Straight Stitches, working two stitches where indicated.

4. When background stitching and Overcasting are completed, work warm brown Straight Stitches on tree branch and cornmeal French Knot on flower. Work remaining embroidery with 6-strand embroidery floss.

5. For tuft, work blue jewel Lark's Head Knot at top of head where indicated. Fray ends to fluff; trim as desired.

6. Stitch front liner/roof support with black and dark sage Continental Stitches where indicated. Do not stitch back liner/roof support.

7. Overcast inside edges of birdhouse front.

8. Place liner/roof supports behind corresponding

birdhouse front and back pieces, aligning with red lines on graphs. Stitch through both layers. Work dark sage Backstitches and eggshell French Knots around opening on front.

9. Work remaining pieces following graphs. Using cornmeal, Overcast top edges of birdhouse front, back and sides, including top edges of liner/roof supports on front and back.

Birdhouse Assembly

1. Using eggshell throughout birdhouse assembly, Whipstitch front and back to sides.

2. Following birdhouse assembly diagram (page 134) through step 5, Whipstitch one each of the following together in order given to form one pedestal side: pedestal insert, upper pedestal side, pedestal insert, lower pedestal side.

3. Repeat three times to form remaining sides of pedestal. Whipstitch four pedestal sides together.

4. Whipstitch top edges of pedestal to inner base and to bottom edges of birdhouse, working through all three layers.

5. Whipstitch unstitched base bottom to bottom of pedestal, filling with aquarium gravel before closing.

6. Glue felt to base bottom and bird to front (see photo); allow to dry.

Roof Assembly

1. Overcast eaves with sea coral between blue dots. Overcast around bottom edges of gables with eggshell from blue dot to blue dot.

2. Follow roof assembly diagram (page 134) through step 3. Matching red stars and orange triangles on graphs and with right sides facing, Whipstitch side edges of gables to eaves with eggshell.

3. Using black, Whipstitch top edges of roof pieces together, catching top edges of eaves in Whipstitching. Whipstitch roof and eaves together around side and bottom edges. ✂

COLOR KEY

Yards	Worsted Weight Yarn
7 (6.5m)	■ Black #12
51 (46.7m)	□ Eggshell #111
30 (27.5m)	□ Cornmeal #220
6 (5.5m)	□ Sea coral #246
29 (26.6m)	□ Maize #261
1 (1m)	▨ Warm brown #336
11 (10.1m)	□ Light sage #631
16 (14.7m)	■ Dark sage #633
2 (1.9m)	□ Pale rose #755
1 (1m)	▨ Cameo rose #759
1 (1m)	□ Pale blue #815
2 (1.9m)	■ Blue jewel #818
	Uncoded background on bluebird is eggshell #111 Continental Stitches
	⁄ Eggshell #111 Straight Stitch
	⁄ Warm brown #336 Straight Stitch
	⁄ Light sage #631 Straight Stitch
	⁄ Dark sage #633 Backstitch and Straight Stitch
	○ Eggshell #111 French Knot
	○ Cornmeal #220 French Knot
	● Blue jewel #818 Lark's Head Knot
	#5 Pearl Cotton
2 (1.9m)	⁄ Black Backstitch and Straight Stitch

Color numbers given are for Coats & Clark Red Heart Classic worsted weight yarn Art. E267.

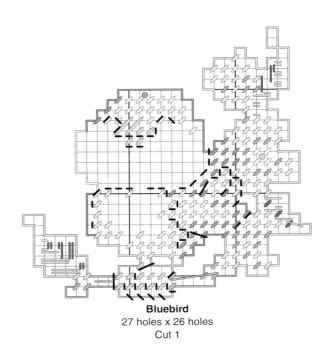

Bluebird
27 holes x 26 holes
Cut 1

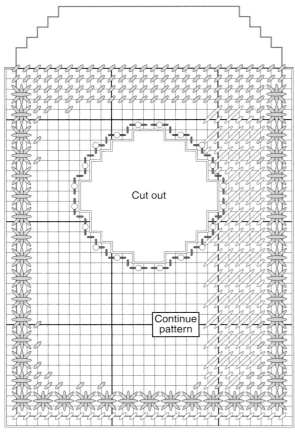

Birdhouse Front
27 holes x 35 holes
Cut 1

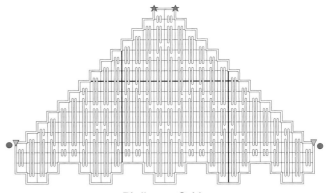

Birdhouse Gable
28 holes x 17 holes
Cut 2

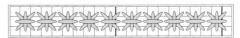

Upper Pedestal Side
21 holes x 3 holes
Cut 4

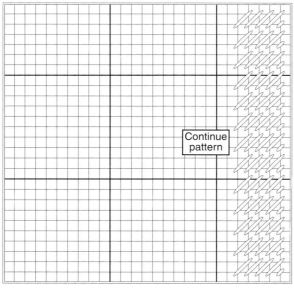

Birdhouse Inner Base
27 holes x 27 holes
Cut 1

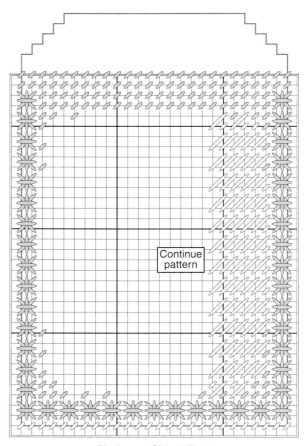

Birdhouse Side & Back
27 holes x 35 holes
Cut 3

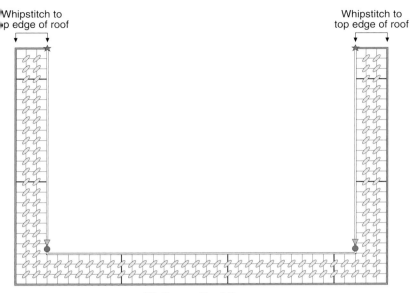

Whipstitch to top edge of roof

Whipstitch to top edge of roof

Birdhouse Roof Eaves
35 holes x 23 holes
Cut 2

Lower Pedestal Side
27 holes x 3 holes
Cut 4

Pedestal Insert
27 holes x 4 holes
Cut 8

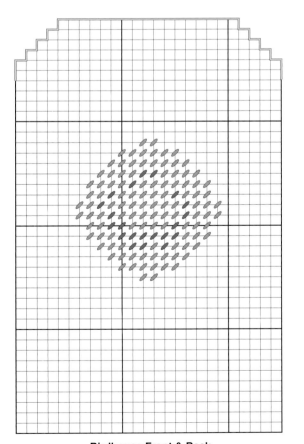

**Birdhouse Front & Back
Liner/Roof Support**
25 holes x 40 holes
Cut 2
Stitch front only

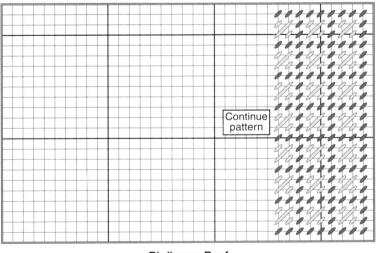

Continue pattern

Birdhouse Roof
35 holes x 23 holes
Cut 2

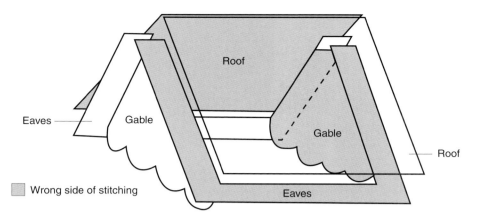

Eaves

Gable

Roof

Gable

Roof

Eaves

Wrong side of stitching

Roof Assembly Diagram

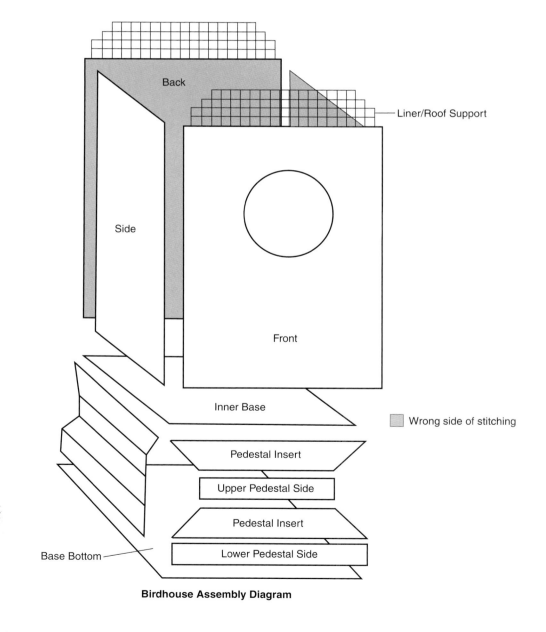

Back

Liner/Roof Support

Side

Front

Inner Base

Wrong side of stitching

Pedestal Insert

Upper Pedestal Side

Pedestal Insert

Base Bottom

Lower Pedestal Side

Birdhouse Assembly Diagram

The Gardener Bunny

This bunny is carefully tending his garden of carrots and might just share a few with you! Design by Lee Lindeman

Skill Level
Beginner

Size
6⅜ inches W x 6 inches H x 3⅝ inches D
(16.2cm x 15.2cm x 9.2cm)

Materials
- 2 sheets 7-count plastic canvas
- Uniek Needloft plastic canvas yarn as listed in color key
- 6-strand embroidery floss as listed in color key
- #16 tapestry needle
- 3½-inch (8.9cm) square 2mm craft foam in desired color or pattern
- 2 (5mm) round black cabochons
- 12mm black animal nose
- ¾-inch (18mm) white pompom
- 3 (¼-inch/0.6cm) flat white buttons
- 4-inch (10.2cm) square wooden base
- Brown acrylic craft paint
- Paintbrush
- 1¾-inch (4.4cm) terra-cotta pot
- 1⅝-inch (4.1cm) basket
- Small piece sandpaper
- Small amount plastic foam
- Fiberfill
- 2¾ inches (7cm) ¼-inch (0.6cm) wooden dowel or craft stick
- Hot-glue gun

Preparation
1. Paint base with brown acrylic paint; allow to dry.

2. Fill terra-cotta pot with plastic foam to about ⅛-inch (0.3cm) from top. For soil, cut sandpaper in a circle to fit over plastic foam inside pot; glue in place.

3. Cut one visor from craft foam, using pattern given (page 137).

Cutting & Stitching

1. Cut plastic canvas according to graphs. Cut one 25-hole x 25-hole piece for grass.

2. Continental Stitch and Overcast grass with fern.

3. Following graphs through step 8, stitch and Overcast pocket with bright blue. Stitch arms with white Continental Stitches, reversing two before stitching.

4. Stitch head front, working uncoded area with white Continental Stitches; stitch head back entirely with white Continental Stitches.

5. Stitch all remaining pieces, working uncoded areas on body pieces with white Continental Stitches.

6. When background stitching is completed, work Backstitches and Straight Stitches on head front, body front and body back with black 6-strand embroidery floss, using 1 ply for whiskers and 6 plies for all remaining embroidery.

7. Using black floss, sew two buttons to body front where indicated on graph.

8. Overcast bottom edges of carrot halves with bittersweet. Using white, Overcast bottom edges of head pieces; Overcast top edges of body front and back, and bottom edges of feet.

Bunny Assembly

1. Using white through step 2, Whipstitch head front and back together around side and top edges, placing fiberfill between and half of dowel or craft stick between.

2. Whipstitch body front and back together along all unstitched edges, placing fiberfill between.

3. Insert remaining half of dowel or craft stick in body, gluing neck of head over neck of body.

4. Whipstitch wrong sides of two arm pieces together. Repeat with remaining arm pieces. Glue shoulders of arms to shoulders of body where indicated on body front graph.

5. Glue pocket to bunny back where indicated on graph with blue shading. Glue white pompom in place for tail. Glue black cabochons to head for eyes. Glue nose in place.

Carrots Assembly

1. For each carrot, cut five lengths of fern yarn; place lengths together on wrong side of one whole carrot piece and one half carrot piece so it appears as though they are coming out the center top of carrot. Glue to secure, making sure to keep glue away from edges.

2. Glue one strand bittersweet to wrong side of whole carrot so it appears as though it is coming out the bottom, making sure to keep glue away from edges.

3. Whipstitch wrong sides of corresponding carrot pieces together, placing fiberfill between and working around fern and bittersweet yarn. Do not Whipstitch bottom edges of half carrot together.

4. For whole carrot, tie fern yarn in a knot next to top edge. For half carrot, wrap a length of fern yarn around fern yarn, beginning at top of carrot until ¾ inch (1.9cm) is wrapped; glue to secure. Fray ends of fern yarn; trim as desired. Unravel bittersweet yarn slightly at bottom of whole carrot.

5. Glue half carrot to center of sandpaper in terra-cotta pot. (See photo.)

Final Assembly

1. Glue grass to top of wooden base. Using photo as a guide through step 3, glue bunny to grass, then glue terra-cotta pot in place to help stabilize bunny.

2. Glue whole carrot and basket to grass.

3. Place visor on bunny's head, wrapping straps around back of head; overlap ends. Glue to secure, then glue button to top strap near end. ✂

Bunny Overall Pocket
6 holes x 5 holes
Cut 1

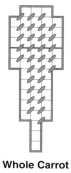

Whole Carrot
5 holes x 14 holes
Cut 2

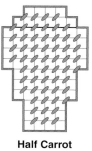

Half Carrot
8 holes x 12 holes
Cut 2

COLOR KEY		
Yards		**Plastic Canvas Yarn**
2 (1.9m)	☐	Pink #07
10 (9.2m)		Fern #23
5 (4.6m)	■	Bittersweet #52
20 (18.3m)	☐	Bright blue #60
45 (41.2m)		Uncoded areas are white #41 Continental Stitches
	∕	White #41 Overcasting and Whipstitching
		6-Strand Embroidery Floss
3 (2.8m)	∕	Black (6-ply) Backstitch and Straight Stitch
	∕	Black (1-ply) Straight Stitch
	○	Attach white button
	●	Attach 5mm black cabochon
	▼	Attach 12mm animal nose
	○	Attach white pompom

Color numbers given are for Uniek Needloft plastic canvas yarn.

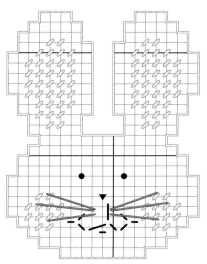

Bunny Head Front & Back
18 holes x 24 holes
Cut 2
Stitch front as graphed
Stitch back entirely with
white Continental Stitches

Bunny Arm
6 holes x 17 holes
Cut 4, reverse 2

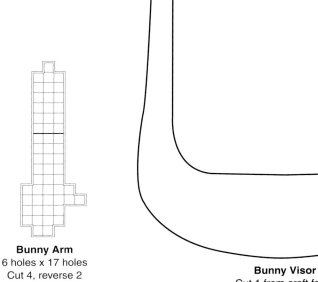

Bunny Visor
Cut 1 from craft foam

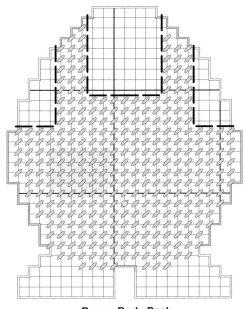

Bunny Body Back
22 holes x 28 holes
Cut 1

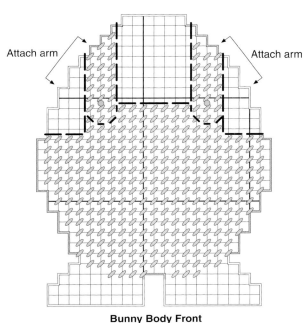

Attach arm

Attach arm

Bunny Body Front
22 holes x 28 holes
Cut 1

Doggie Welcome

Keep doors propped open and greet your guests with this adorable puppy doorstop. He'll cheerfully play the welcoming committee for you! Design by Debbie Tabor

Skill Level
Beginner

Size
6⅜ inches W x 6 inches H x 3⅝ inches D
(16.2cm x 15.2cm x 9.2cm)

Materials
- 1 sheet 7-count plastic canvas
- Worsted weight yarn as listed in color key
- 6-strand embroidery floss as listed in color key
- #16 tapestry needle
- Weighted stuffing pellets
- Hot-glue gun

Instructions

1. Cut plastic canvas according to graphs, carefully cutting canvas apart where indicated with blue lines.

2. Cut one 10-hole x 25-hole piece for doorstop top, one 10-hole x 14-hole piece for doorstop back and one 10-hole x piece 21-hole for doorstop base. Base will remain unstitched.

3. Stitch and Overcast doggie and bone following graphs, working uncoded background on doggie with bronze Continental Stitches and uncoded background on bone with off-white Continental Stitches.

4. When background stitching and Overcasting are completed, use white yarn to work Straight Stitch on nose and French Knots on eyes. Work all remaining embroidery with black 6-strand embroidery floss.

5. With right sides facing front, slip bone in doggie's mouth and glue in place (see photo). Set aside.

6. Stitch doorstop top and back with white Continental Stitches. Stitch one doorstop side as graphed; reverse remaining side before stitching.

7. Following Fig. 1 and using white throughout, Whipstitch top to angled edges of sides. Whipstitch sides and top to base, then Whipstitch sides, top and base to back, filling with weighted stuffing pellets before closing.

8. Center and glue doorstop back to wrong side of doggie. ✂

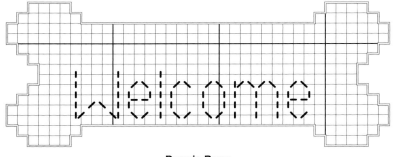

Doggie Bone
36 holes x 14 holes
Cut 1

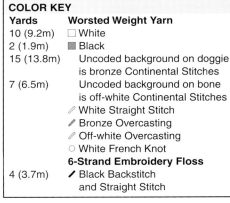

COLOR KEY

Yards	Worsted Weight Yarn
10 (9.2m)	☐ White
2 (1.9m)	■ Black
15 (13.8m)	Uncoded background on doggie is bronze Continental Stitches
7 (6.5m)	Uncoded background on bone is off-white Continental Stitches
	⁄ White Straight Stitch
	⁄ Bronze Overcasting
	⁄ Off-white Overcasting
	○ White French Knot
	6-Strand Embroidery Floss
4 (3.7m)	⁄ Black Backstitch and Straight Stitch

Doorstop Side
21 holes x 14 holes
Cut 2, reverse 1

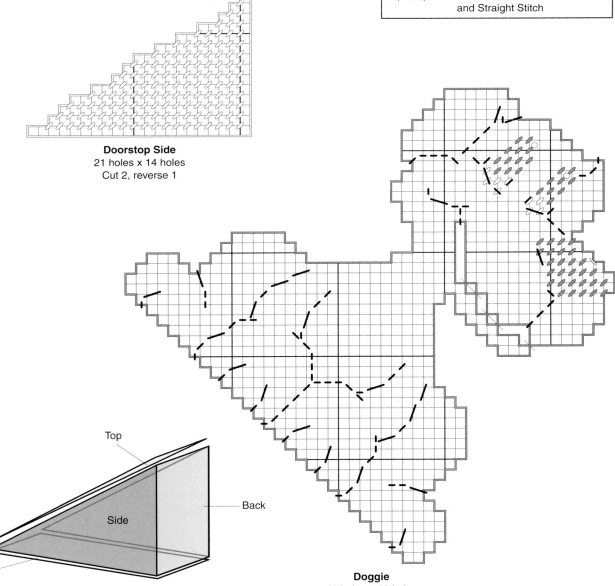

**Fig. 1
Doorstop Assembly Diagram**

Top
Back
Side
Base

Doggie
46 holes x 46 holes
Cut 1
Carefully cut apart at blue lines

Sweet Liberty

Decked out in red, white and blue, this little shelf-sitter will help you let your patriotic pride shine. Design by Debra Arch

Skill Level
Intermediate

Size
7 inches W x 9½ inches H x 7 inches D
(17.8cm x 24.1cm x 17.8cm), including crown

Materials
- 2 sheets 7-count plastic canvas
- 2 (4-inch) Uniek QuickShape plastic canvas radial circles
- 2 (6-inch) Uniek QuickShape plastic canvas radial circles
- 2 (9-inch) Uniek QuickShape plastic canvas radial circles
- Coats & Clark Red Heart Classic worsted weight yarn Art. E267 as listed in color key
- Coats & Clark Red Heart Super Saver worsted weight yarn Art. E300 as listed in color key
- Kreinik ⅛-inch Ribbon as listed in color key
- #16 tapestry needle
- 2 (5mm) round black cabochons
- 1-inch (2.5cm) silver liberty bell
- ½-inch (1.3cm) silver star
- 9⅛-inch-tall (23.3cm) empty potato chip canister with lid
- 2 cups sand
- Light rose powder blush
- Cotton swab or small paintbrush
- Hot-glue gun

Cutting & Stitching
1. Cut body and collar from 7-count plastic canvas according to graphs (pages 144 and 145).

2. Cut body top and base from 4-inch radial circles, two arms from 6-inch radial circles and two star crowns from 9-inch radial circles (pages 142 and 143), cutting away gray areas. Body base will remain unstitched.

3. Stitch and Overcast collar, working cherry red Backstitches when background stitching and Overcasting are completed.

4. Stitch body following graph, working uncoded face area on body with eggshell Continental Stitches and using a double strand linen yarn for Straight Stitching hair.

5. Stitch remaining pieces following graphs, reversing one star crown before stitching.

Assembly
1. Fill potato chip canister with sand and securely glue on lid. Whipstitch side edges of body together, forming a cylinder, then Whipstitch body top in place. Place body over canister, then Whipstitch base to bottom edge of body.

2. Using photo as a guide through step 7, Overlap front ends of collar and tack together with white yarn. Make a small bow with cherry red yarn and glue to top of overlap.

3. Slip collar over head and glue center back of collar to back seam at bottom of hairline. Glue overlap at center front where bodice meets skirt.

4. Matching shoulder edges, fold one arm in half at hand with wrong sides together, then Whipstitch halves together all around, forming one arm. Repeat with second arm. Butt two hands together and tack securely together behind hands with eggshell yarn.

5. Glue shoulders of arms under collar so that hands are under collar on front. Glue silver liberty bell behind hands. Glue silver star in front of hands at top of bell.

6. Matching edges, Whipstitch wrong sides of star crown pieces together with silver ribbon. Slide crown over head at an angle; glue in place.

7. Glue cabochons in place for eyes. Using cotton swab or small paintbrush, apply a light amount of blush to cheeks. ✂

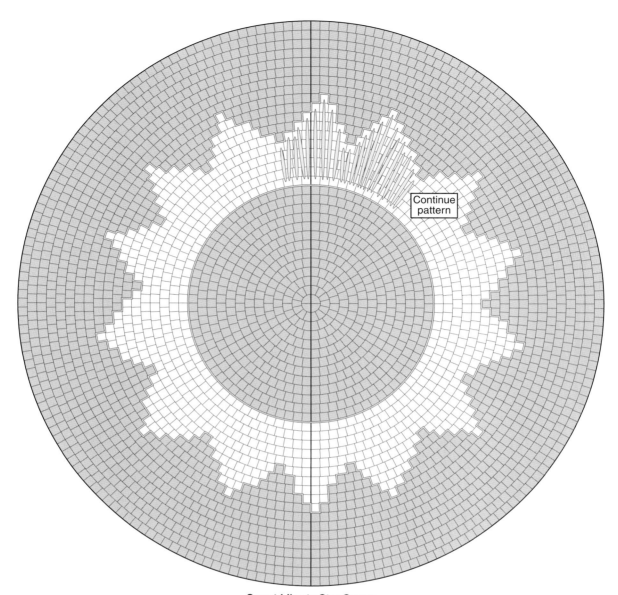

Continue pattern

Sweet Liberty Star Crown
Cut 2, reverse 1,
from 9¼-inch radial circles,
cutting away gray areas

COLOR KEY	
Yards	**Worsted Weight Yarn**
35 (32m)	☐ White #1
10 (9.2m)	☐ Eggshell #111
20 (18.3m)	■ Soft navy #853
25 (22.9m)	■ Cherry red #912
	Uncoded area on face is eggshell #111 Continental Stitches
30 (27.5m)	✎ Linen #330 Straight Stitch and Whipstitching
	✎ Cherry red #912 Backstitch
⅛-Inch Ribbon	
35 (32m)	☐ Silver Hi Lustre #001HL
	● Attach black cabochon

Color numbers given are for Coats & Clark Red Heart Classic worsted weight yarn Art. E267 and Super Saver worsted weight yarn Art. E300 and Kreinik ⅛-inch Ribbon.

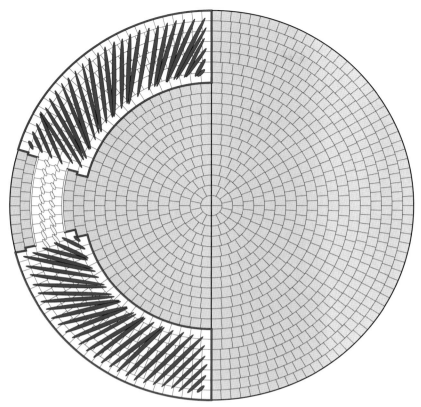

Sweet Liberty Arm
Cut 2 from 6-inch radial circles,
cutting away gray areas

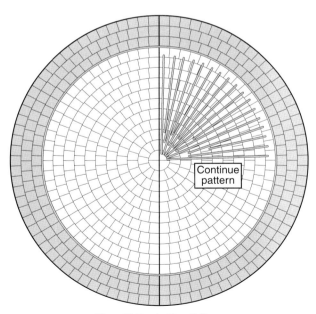

Continue
pattern

Sweet Liberty Top & Base
Cut 2 from 4-inch radial circles,
cutting away gray area
Stitch top only

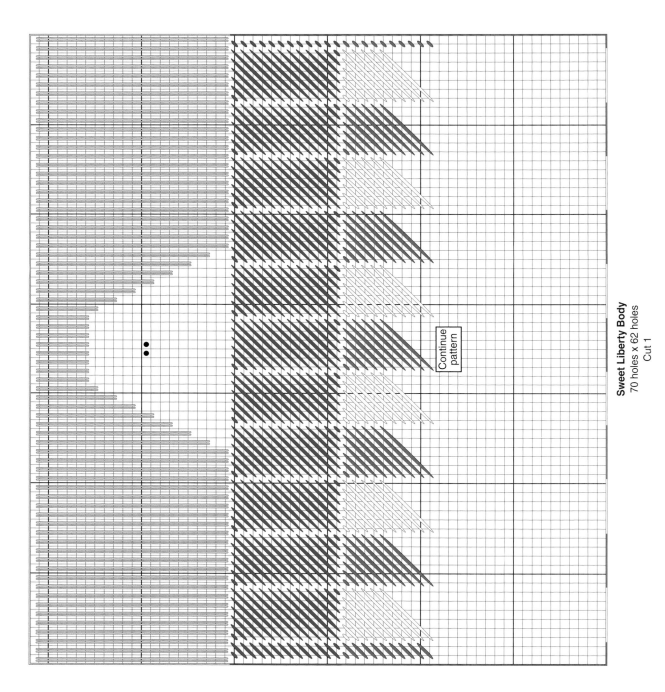

Sweet Liberty Body
70 holes x 62 holes
Cut 1

Continue
pattern

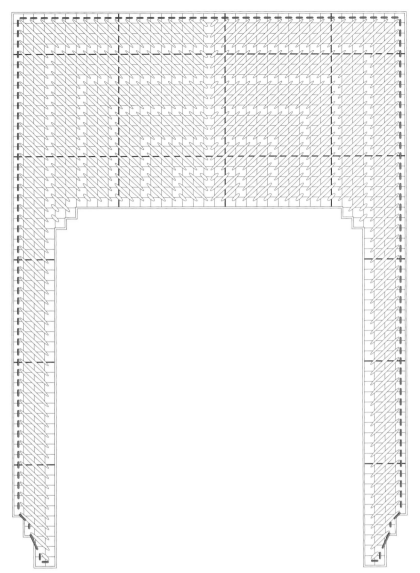

Sweet Liberty Collar
37 holes x 54 holes
Cut 1

COLOR KEY	
Yards	**Worsted Weight Yarn**
35 (32m)	☐ White #1
10 (9.2m)	☐ Eggshell #111
20 (18.3m)	■ Soft navy #853
25 (22.9m)	■ Cherry red #912
	Uncoded area on face is eggshell #111 Continental Stitches
30 (27.5m)	⁄ Linen #330 Straight Stitch and Whipstitching
	⁄ Cherry red #912 Backstitch
	¹⁄₈-Inch Ribbon
35 (32m)	☐ Silver Hi Lustre #001HL
	● Attach black cabochon
Color numbers given are for Coats & Clark Red Heart Classic worsted weight yarn Art. E267 and Super Saver worsted weight yarn Art. E300 and Kreinik ¹⁄₈-inch Ribbon.	

Grandma's Favorite Chair

This fancy old-fashioned chair doubles as a handy pincushion and a darling addition to your decor. Design by Terry Ricioli

Skill Level
Intermediate

Size
4 inches W x 6⅛ inches H x 2⅝ inches D
(10.2cm x 15.6cm x 6.7cm)

Materials
- 1 sheet 7-count plastic canvas
- Uniek Needloft plastic canvas yarn as listed in color key

- #16 tapestry needle
- 4 (10mm x 30mm) wooden beads
- 6-inch (15.2cm) blue felt circle
- Small amount fiberfill
- Hand-sewing needle
- Blue sewing thread
- Hot-glue gun

Cutting & Stitching

1. Cut plastic canvas according to graphs. Cut one 20-hole x 15-hole piece for chair bottom. Chair bottom will remain unstitched.

2. Continental Stitch chair front with sail blue. Stitch pieces following graphs, reversing one side and one side liner before stitching.

3. With wrong sides facing, Whipstitch sides to back from blue dot to blue dot. Whipstitch front to sides from black arrows to red arrows.

4. Whipstitch bottom to front, back and sides; Overcast top edge of front.

5. With right sides facing, Whipstitch back liner to side liners from yellow dot to red dot.

6. With wrong sides facing, place liner pieces and chair back and sides together, matching top and side edges. Whipstitch together around side and top edges from red arrow to red arrow. Bottom edges of liner pieces will remain unstitched.

7. For chair seat/pincushion, using hand-sewing needle and blue thread, run a gathering stitch near outside edge of felt circle. Pull thread to gather, stuffing firmly with fiberfill. Check fit and adjust as needed; glue in place.

8. For chair legs, glue wooden beads to chair bottom at corners. ✂

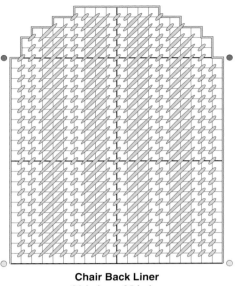

Chair Back Liner
20 holes x 25 holes
Cut 1

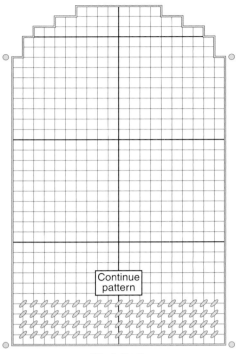

Continue pattern

Chair Back
20 holes x 33 holes
Cut 1

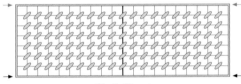

Chair Front
20 holes x 7 holes
Cut 1

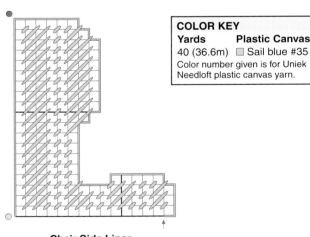

Chair Side Liner
15 holes x 19 holes
Cut 2, reverse 1

COLOR KEY

Yards	Plastic Canvas Yarn
40 (36.6m)	▢ Sail blue #35

Color number given is for Uniek
Needloft plastic canvas yarn.

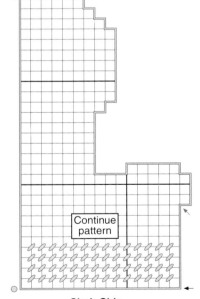

Continue pattern

Chair Side
16 holes x 28 holes
Cut 2, reverse 1

Delightful Tissue Covers

Just right for any room, tissue toppers can be displayed year-round. Featuring a variety of motifs, this chapter is filled with darling toppers in assorted sizes and styles.

Summer Floral Explosion

Colorful plastic canvas and bright colors of yarn combine for a floral topper you can't resist! Petals and leaves give this piece dimension. Design by Terry Ricioli

Skill Level
Beginner

Size
Fits boutique-size tissue box

Materials
- 1½ sheets turquoise 7-count plastic canvas
- 1 sheet clear 7-count plastic canvas
- Uniek Needloft plastic canvas yarn as listed in color key

- #16 tapestry needle
- Hot-glue gun

Cutting & Stitching
1. Cut sides and top from turquoise plastic canvas; cut flowers, petals and leaves from clear plastic canvas according to graphs (pages 151 and 152).

2. Stitch sides and top following graphs, securing tails behind stitching so extra yarn does not show through canvas. Overcast inside edges of top, and bottom edges of sides.

3. Stitch 32 petals with bright yellow as graphed. Stitch remaining eight petals, replacing bright yellow with bright orange. Overcast around side and top edges from dot to dot.

4. Stitch and Overcast remaining pieces following graphs.

Assembly
1. Using bright orange, Whipstitch bottom edges of bright orange petals to top where indicated with orange lines.

2. Using bright yellow, Whipstitch bottom edges of bright yellow petals around orange flowers on sides where indicated with blue lines.

3. Using holly, tack leaves to stem of large orange flower on each side where indicated with green dots.

4. Using photo as a guide through step 5, glue centers of purple flowers and small orange flowers in place.

5. For each side, glue one small orange flower to top of second holly stem, one purple flower to top of second bright green stem and one pink flower center (stitched with bright purple) to center of pink flower.

6. Using turquoise, Whipstitch sides together, then Whipstitch sides to top. ✂

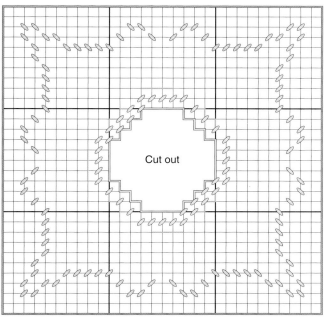

Summer Floral Explosion Top
30 holes x 30 holes
Cut 1 from turquoise

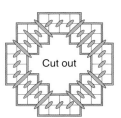

Summer Floral Explosions Orange Flower
10 holes x 10 holes
Cut 4 from clear

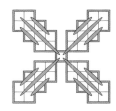

Summer Floral Explosions Purple Flower
9 holes x 9 holes
Cut 4 from clear

Summer Floral Explosions Orange Flower Center
5 holes x 5 holes
Cut 4 from clear

Summer Floral Explosions Purple Flower Center
3 holes x 3 holes
Cut 4 from clear

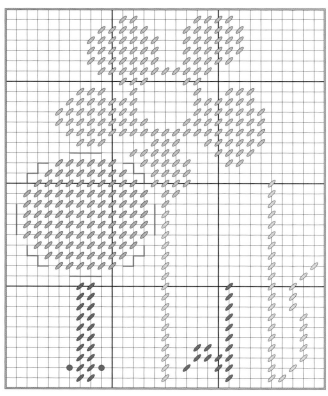

Summer Floral Explosion Side
30 holes x 37 holes
Cut 4 from turquoise

**Summer Floral Explosions
Pink Flower Center**
4 holes x 4 holes
Cut 4 from clear

Summer Floral Explosions Leaf
7 holes x 3 holes
Cut 8 from clear

COLOR KEY	
Yards	**Plastic Canvas Yarn**
6 (5.5m)	■ Holly #27
20 (18.3m)	▨ Bright orange #58
10 (9.2m)	▨ Bright green #61
12 (11m)	▨ Bright pink #62
18 (16.5m)	☐ Bright yellow #62
8 (7.4m)	▨ Bright purple #63
6 (5.5m)	╱ Turquoise #54 Overcasting and Whipstitching

Color numbers given are for Uniek Needloft plastic canvas yarn.

Summer Floral Explosions Petal
5 holes x 4 holes
Cut 40 from clear
Stitch 32 as graphed
Stitch 8 replacing bright
yellow with bright orange

Picnic Guest

Cute as a bug, you won't mind this little guy at your next picnic! Mimicking a picnic basket, this whimsical tissue topper is fun year-round. Design by Mary T. Cosgrove

Skill Level
Intermediate

Size
Fits regular-size tissue box

Materials
- 2 sheets 7-count plastic canvas
- Uniek Needloft plastic canvas yarn as listed in color key
- #16 tapestry needle
- 2 (10mm) movable eyes
- 12-inch (30.5cm) black chenille stem
- 2 sheets yellow felt
- Fabric glue

Cutting & Stitching

1. Cut plastic canvas according to graphs (pages 154, 155 and 156). Cut two 4-hole x 18-hole pieces for bread crusts and two 4-hole x 7-hole pieces for watermelon sides.

2. Cut one 9½-inch x 5 inch (24.1 cm x 12.7cm) piece and one 9½-inch x 4½-inch (24.1 cm x 11.4cm) piece from yellow felt.

3. Stitch and Overcast ant and napkin following graphs. Work red Backstitches for mouth on ant.

4. Continental Stitch bread crusts with maple and watermelon sides with Christmas green.

5. Stitch remaining pieces following graphs, working uncoded areas on watermelon pieces with red Continental Stitches and leaving green, red and maple Whipstitch lines and uncoded areas on topper top unworked at this time.

6. Overcast lid around side and top edges. Overcast inside edges of topper top.

Ant Assembly

1. Cut black chenille stem into six 2-inch (5.1cm) lengths. Wrap two around edge at head top where indicated for antennae; curl ends.

2. Attach remaining four where indicated for legs, bending as desired.

3. Attach a length of red yarn to one corner of napkin where indicated with red dot. Bring length around back of ant's neck and thread through other corner of napkin with red dot. Pull to curve napkin slightly. Secure ends on wrong side.

4. Glue movable eyes to head (see photo).

Top Assembly

1. For watermelon, Whipstitch long edges of sides to front and back with Christmas green, then Whipstitch front, back and sides to watermelon top with adjacent colors.

2. Using adjacent colors, Whipstitch bottom edges of assembled watermelon to topper top along red Whipstitch lines.

3. Using maple, Whipstitch short edges of bread crusts together forming an "L" shape, then Whipstitch straight edges of bread pieces to crusts.

4. Using adjacent colors, Whipstitch unworked edges of bread to topper top along light brown Whipstitch lines.

Tissue Topper Assembly

1. Whipstitch topper front and back to sides; Overcast bottom edges.

2. Overcast top and bottom edges of handles. Using Christmas green, Whipstitch ends of one handle to each side where indicated with green dots.

3. Whipstitch top to front, back and sides.

Finishing

1. Whipstitch bottom edge of lid to topper top along green Whipstitch line.

2. Using black, Whipstitch bottom edge of ant to top in front of lid where indicated with black dots; tack back of ant to lid.

3. Glue large piece of felt to back of lid, then glue smaller piece to sides and bottom of first piece, forming a pocket. ✂

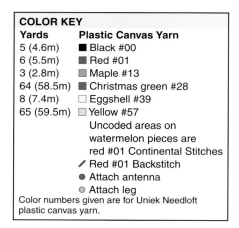

COLOR KEY

Yards	Plastic Canvas Yarn
5 (4.6m)	■ Black #00
6 (5.5m)	■ Red #01
3 (2.8m)	■ Maple #13
64 (58.5m)	■ Christmas green #28
8 (7.4m)	□ Eggshell #39
65 (59.5m)	□ Yellow #57
	Uncoded areas on watermelon pieces are red #01 Continental Stitches
╱	Red #01 Backstitch
●	Attach antenna
○	Attach leg

Color numbers given are for Uniek Needloft plastic canvas yarn.

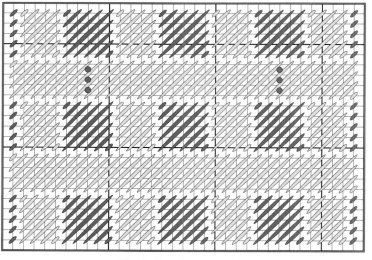

Picnic Guest Topper Side
34 holes x 24 holes
Cut 2

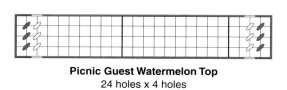

Picnic Guest Watermelon Top
24 holes x 4 holes
Cut 1

Picnic Guest Topper Handle
24 holes x 3 holes
Cut 2

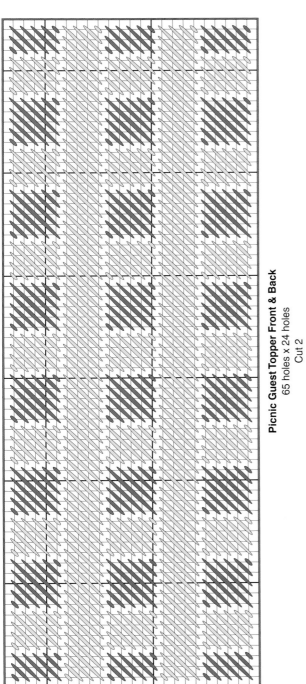

Picnic Guest Topper Front & Back
65 holes x 24 holes
Cut 2

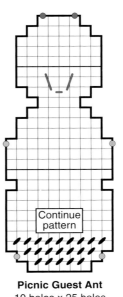

Picnic Guest Ant
10 holes x 25 holes
Cut 1

Continue
pattern

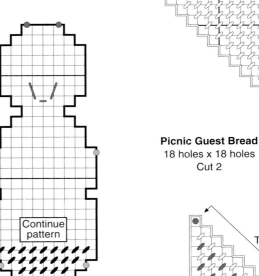

Picnic Guest Bread
18 holes x 18 holes
Cut 2

Top

Picnic Guest Napkin
9 holes x 9 holes
Cut 1

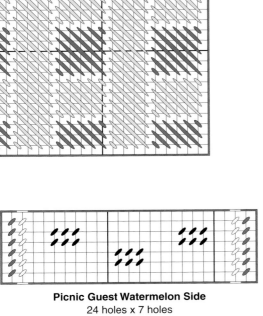

Picnic Guest Watermelon Side
24 holes x 7 holes
Cut 2

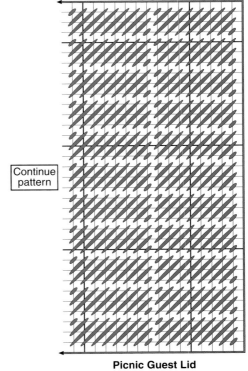

Continue
pattern

Picnic Guest Lid
65 holes x 34 holes
Cut 1

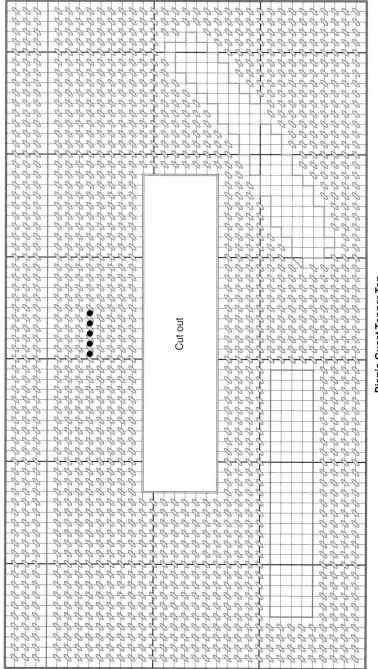

Picnic Guest Topper Top
65 holes x 34 holes
Cut 1

Cut out

Red Hat Style

Pretty beads add flair to this purse-shaped tissue topper that celebrates the red-hat lifestyle. Design by Debra Arch

Skill Level
Beginner

Size
Fits boutique-size tissue box

Materials
- 3 sheets 7-count plastic canvas
- Uniek Needloft plastic canvas yarn as listed in color key
- Kreinik ⅛-inch Ribbon as listed in color key
- #16 tapestry needle
- 204 (4mm) round dark purple beads
- Hand-sewing needle
- Purple sewing thread
- Hot-glue gun

Instructions

1. Cut plastic canvas according to graphs (pages 158, 159 and 160).

2. Using a single strand Christmas red yarn, stitch and Overcast handle. Stitch remaining pieces, following graphs, using a double strand (not graphed as double) Christmas red yarn to stitch front, back and sides.

3. Overcast around side and bottom edges of clasp pieces from blue dot to blue dot. Overcast clasp lock.

4. Using hand-sewing needle and purple sewing thread, attach beads to handle, front, back, sides and clasp lock where indicated on graphs.

5. Whipstitch top pieces together between brackets, forming opening for tissue. Whipstitch edges of opening.

6. Whipstitch front and back to sides; Overcast bottom edges. Whipstitch top to sides only.

7. Align top edges of top and clasp pieces to top edges of front and back. *Note: Front and back will each be sandwiched between clasp and top.* Whipstitch together through all three layers.

8. Using photo as a guide, glue handle and clasp lock in place. ✄

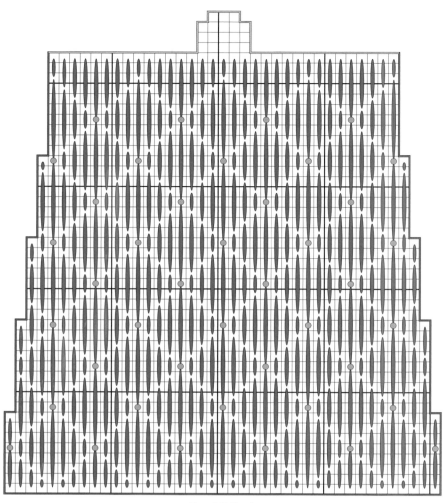

Front & Back
41 holes x 47 holes
Cut 2

COLOR KEY	
Yards	**Plastic Canvas Yarn**
170 (155.5m)	■ Christmas red #02
14 (12.9m)	■ Purple #46
	⅛-Inch Ribbon
3 (2.8m)	■ Silver #001
	● Attach purple bead
Color numbers given are for Uniek Needloft plastic canvas yarn and Kreinik ⅛-inch Ribbon.	

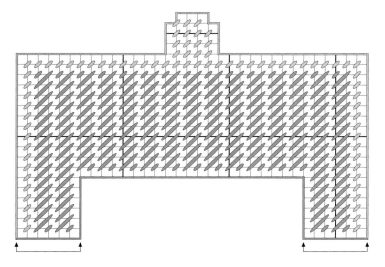

Top
33 holes x 22 holes
Cut 2

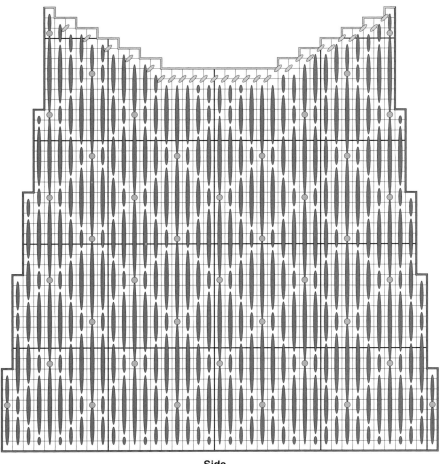

Side
41 holes x 43 holes
Cut 2

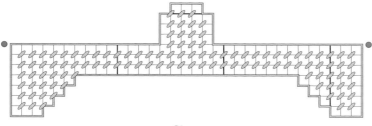

Clasp
33 holes x 11 holes
Cut 2

Clasp Lock
8 holes x 8 holes
Cut 1

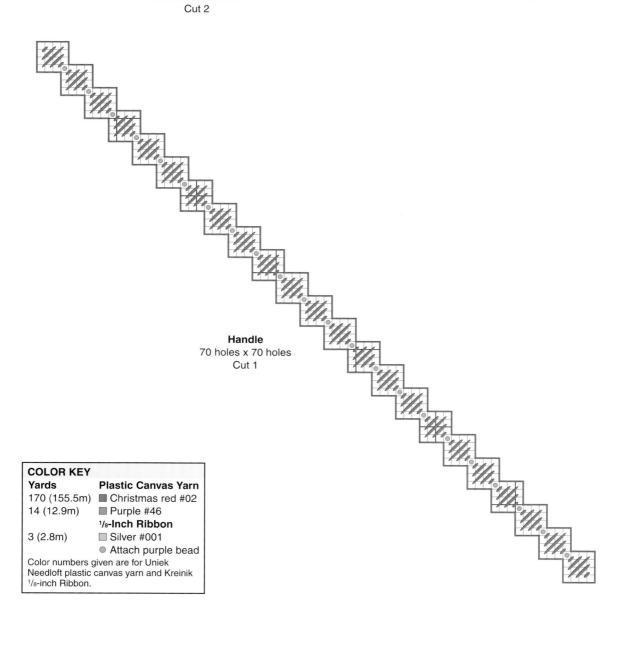

Handle
70 holes x 70 holes
Cut 1

COLOR KEY

Yards	Plastic Canvas Yarn
170 (155.5m)	■ Christmas red #02
14 (12.9m)	■ Purple #46
	⅛-Inch Ribbon
3 (2.8m)	■ Silver #001
	● Attach purple bead

Color numbers given are for Uniek
Needloft plastic canvas yarn and Kreinik
⅛-inch Ribbon.

Cute Kitten

Amuse any cat lover with this whimsical kitty who is so cheery she doesn't even notice the tiny mouse frolicking on her tail!

Design by Michele Wilcox

Skill Level
Beginner

Size
Fits boutique-size tissue box

Materials
- 2 sheets 7-count plastic canvas
- Uniek Needloft plastic canvas yarn as listed in color key
- #3 pearl cotton as listed in color key
- #16 tapestry needle
- 2 (¼-inch/0.6cm) black buttons
- Hand-sewing needle
- Black sewing thread
- Hot-glue gun

Instructions
1. Cut plastic canvas according to graphs (pages 162 and 163).

2. Following graphs throughout, stitch and Overcast kitten head, tail, legs, mouse and mouse ears, reversing one front leg and one hind leg before stitching. Stitch top and sides.

3. When background stitching is completed, work black pearl cotton Backstitches on kitten head and French Knots on mouse head. Using hand-sewing needle and black sewing thread, sew buttons to eyes on kitten head where indicated.

4. Using tangerine, Overcast inside edges of top and bottom edges of sides; Whipstitch sides together, then Whipstitch sides to top.

5. For mouse tail, cut a 1½ to 2-inch (3.8cm to 5.1cm) length gray yarn. Glue to wrong side of mouse where indicated on graph.

6. Using photo as a guide through step 7 and making sure bottom edges are even, glue front legs and head to topper front; glue hind legs to sides. Glue kitten tail to center top of back.

7. Glue ears to mouse, then glue mouse to kitten's tail. ✂

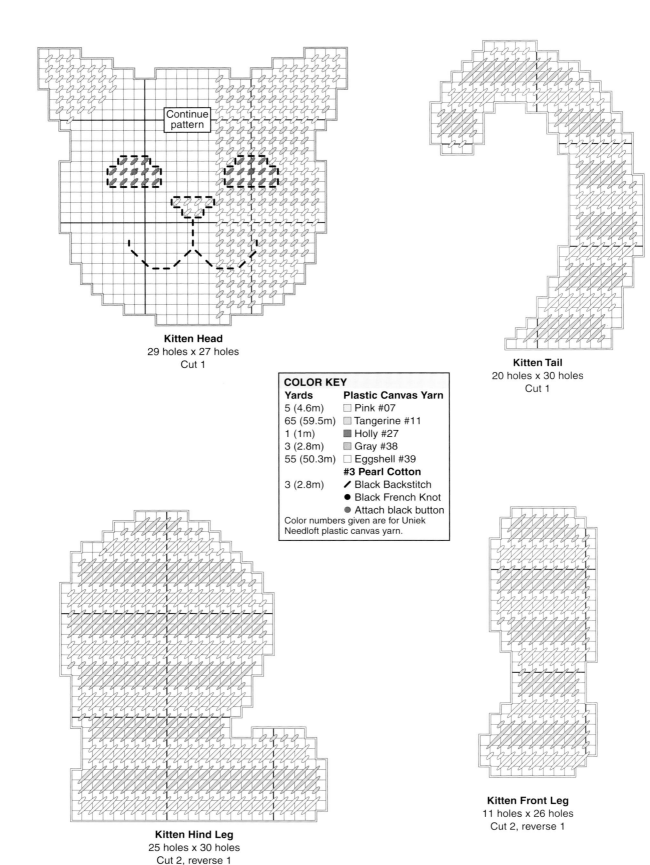

Kitten Head
29 holes x 27 holes
Cut 1

Continue
pattern

Kitten Tail
20 holes x 30 holes
Cut 1

COLOR KEY

Yards	Plastic Canvas Yarn
5 (4.6m)	☐ Pink #07
65 (59.5m)	☐ Tangerine #11
1 (1m)	■ Holly #27
3 (2.8m)	☐ Gray #38
55 (50.3m)	☐ Eggshell #39
#3 Pearl Cotton	
3 (2.8m)	✓ Black Backstitch
	● Black French Knot
	● Attach black button

Color numbers given are for Uniek
Needloft plastic canvas yarn.

Kitten Hind Leg
25 holes x 30 holes
Cut 2, reverse 1

Kitten Front Leg
11 holes x 26 holes
Cut 2, reverse 1

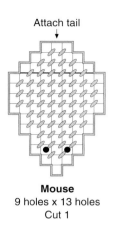

Attach tail

Mouse
9 holes x 13 holes
Cut 1

Mouse Ear
4 holes x 4 holes
Cut 2

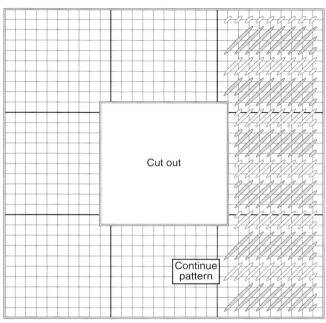

Cut out

Continue
pattern

Cute Kitten Top
30 holes x 30 holes
Cut 1

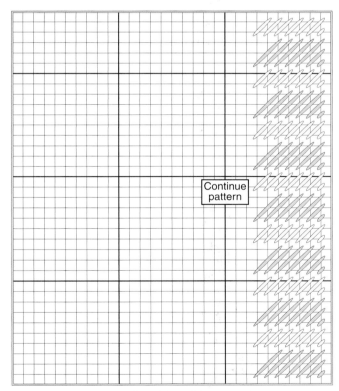

Continue
pattern

Cute Kitten Side
30 holes x 36 holes
Cut 4

Best Friend

Keep tissues close at hand with this happy hound that would rather sleep than chase rabbits. Design by Christina Laws

Skill Level
Beginner

Size
Fits family-size tissue box

Materials
- 3 sheets 7-count plastic canvas
- Worsted weight yarn as listed in color key
- #16 tapestry needle
- Hot-glue gun

Instructions

1. Cut plastic canvas according to graphs (this page and pages 166 and 167). Cut two 34-hole x 28-hole pieces for topper sides.

2. Stitch sides with medium brown Continental Stitches. Following graphs throughout stitching, stitch and Overcast paws. Stitch topper back and top.

3. Stitch hound front, working uncoded areas with white Continental Stitches. Reverse hound back and stitch around outside of blue lines with tan and white Reverse Continental Stitches. Do not stitch inside blue lines.

4. When background stitching on hound front is completed, use full strand yarn to work Black Backstitches and Straight Stitches. Use two strands yarn to work dark brown Backstitches.

5. Using medium brown throughout, Whipstitch top and sides together, then Whipstitch top and sides to right side of hound back along blue lines only. Whipstitch top and sides to topper back.

6. Following graph, Whipstitch hound front to hound back around all edges, catching topper side below ear on right while Whipstitching.

7. Overcast all remaining edges with medium brown. ✂

Best Friend Topper Back
65 holes x 28 holes
Cut 1

Continue pattern

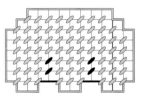

Best Friend Paw
12 holes x 8 holes
Cut 2

COLOR KEY	
Yards	**Worsted Weight Yarn**
70 (64m)	▨ Medium brown
15 (13.8m)	☐ White
2 (1.9m)	■ Black
	Uncoded areas on hound are white Continental Stitches
2 (1.9m)	⁄ Dark brown (2-ply) Backstitch
	⁄ Black (4-ply) Backstitch and Straight Stitch

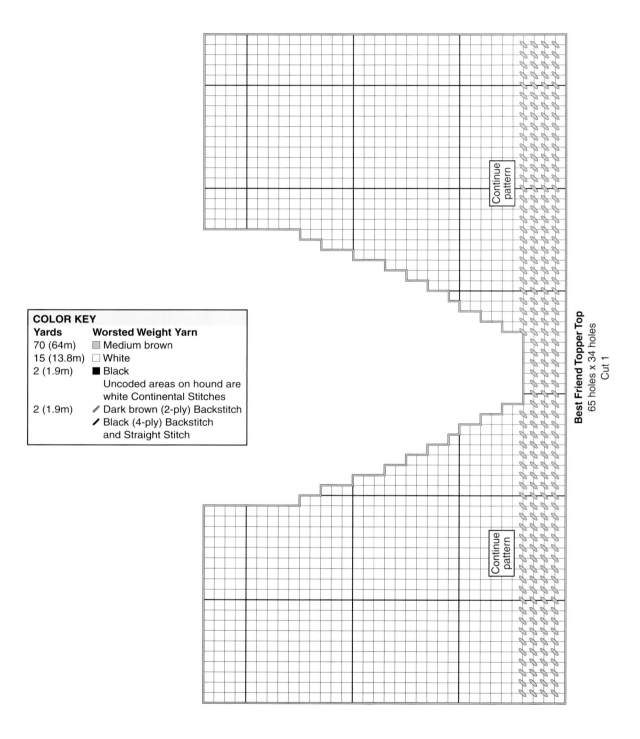

COLOR KEY

Yards	Worsted Weight Yarn
70 (64m)	▨ Medium brown
15 (13.8m)	☐ White
2 (1.9m)	■ Black
	Uncoded areas on hound are white Continental Stitches
2 (1.9m)	╱ Dark brown (2-ply) Backstitch
	╱ Black (4-ply) Backstitch and Straight Stitch

Continue pattern

Continue pattern

Best Friend Topper Top
65 holes x 34 holes
Cut 1

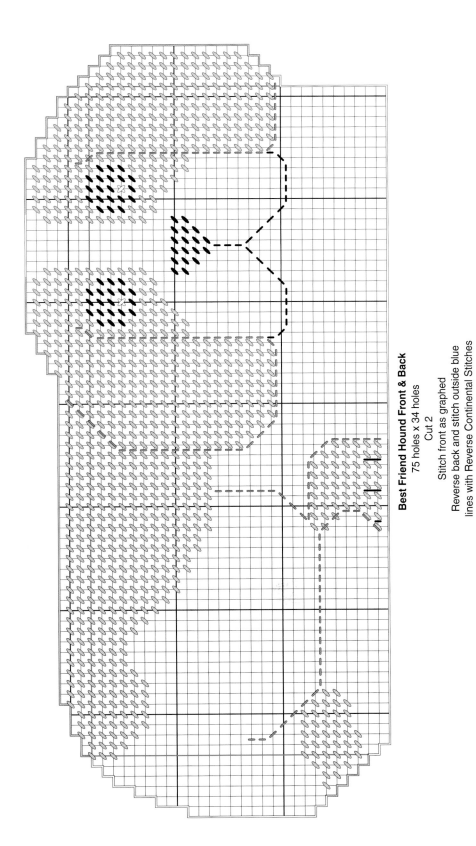

Best Friend Hound Front & Back
75 holes x 34 holes
Cut 2
Stitch front as graphed
Reverse back and stitch outside blue
lines with Reverse Continental Stitches

Kitchen Chicken

Rise and shine to this adorable hen watching over your roost. The napkin caddy holds salt and pepper shakers for convenience, and the tissue topper coordinates perfectly. Designs by Janelle Giese

Skill Level
Intermediate

Size
Tissue Topper: Fits boutique-style tissue box
Napkin and Shaker Caddy: 8⅛ inches W x 6¾ inches H x 4⅝ inches D (20.6cm x 17.1cm x 11.7cm)
Chicken Motif: 5½ inches W x 5⅝ inches H (14 cm x 14.3cm)

Materials
- 3½ sheets regular 7-count plastic canvas
- 2 sheets stiff 7-count plastic canvas
- Uniek Needloft plastic canvas yarn as listed in color key
- #3 pearl cotton as listed in color key
- #5 pearl cotton as listed in color key
- #16 tapestry needle
- ¾ cup aquarium gravel
- Thick white glue

Chickens
1. Cut two chickens from regular plastic canvas according to graph (page 170).

2. Stitch and Overcast pieces following graph, working uncoded background with white Continental Stitches.

3. When background stitching and Overcasting are completed, use a full strand yarn to embroider accents on beaks, tails, wings and nests. Use full strand yarn to work two Straight Stitches for pupils of each eye.

4. Work #5 pearl cotton embroidery next. To complete embroidery, use 1 ply white yarn to Straight Stitch each eye highlight, coming up at top corner and going down between black Straight Stitches where indicated.

Tissue Topper
1. Cut one front, three sides and one top from regular plastic canvas according to graphs (pages 171 and 172).

2. Stitch pieces following graphs. When background stitching is completed, work black #3 pearl cotton Backstitches across bands on sides.

3. Using black yarn throughout, Overcast inside edges of top and bottom edges of sides. Whipstitch front and sides together, then Whipstitch front and sides to top.

4. Center and glue one chicken to front, making sure bottom edges are even.

Caddy Cutting & Stitching
1. Cut two shaker rings from regular plastic canvas; cut one front, one back, two bases and two sides from stiff plastic canvas according to graphs (pages 170, 171 and 172).

2. From stiff plastic canvas, also cut one 31-hole x 13 hole piece for napkin rest and two 31-hole x 27-hole pieces for caddy supports.

3. Stitch napkin rest with black yarn Continental Stitches. Stitch sides and shaker rings following graphs, overlapping each shaker ring where indicated before stitching. Overcast top edges of rings with red.

4. Place one caddy support piece each behind caddy front and back, aligning top and side edges. Stitch pieces following graphs, working through both layers where supports are aligned and leaving blue Whipstitch lines unworked at this time.

5. Place caddy base pieces together and stitch as one, leaving blue and red Whipstitch lines unworked at this time. Turn base over and Continental Stitch center of base (shaded green) on wrong side.

6. When background stitching is completed, Backstitch bands on back, sides and rings with black #3 pearl cotton.

Caddy Assembly

1. Use black yarn throughout assembly. Use Continental Stitches to Whipstitch long edges of napkin rest to front and back along blue Whipstitch lines, catching bottom edge of support on each while Whipstitching.

2. Whipstitch sides to front, back and napkin rest. Overcast remaining edges of front and back using 1½-yard (1.4m) lengths for each.

3. Placing Overlap on each ring in back, Whipstitch bottom edges of rings to circles in front, including bars indicated with red lines.

4. Whipstitch caddy front and sides to base, including bars indicated with blue lines, leaving back edge unworked. Fill base with aquarium gravel through back opening, then Whipstitch back edge closed.

5. Using photo as a guide, center and glue chicken to caddy front. ✄

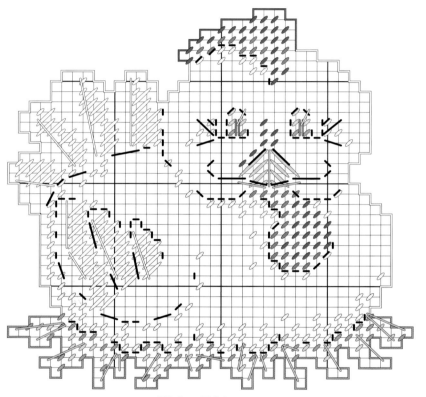

Kitchen Chicken
38 holes x 37 holes
Cut 2 from regular

COLOR KEY	
Yards	**Plastic Canvas Yarn**
42 (38.4m)	■ Black #00
4 (3.7m)	■ Red #01
1 (1m)	■ Burgundy #03
3 (2.8m)	□ Eggshell #39
2 (1.9m)	■ Beige #40
46 (42.1m)	□ White #41
3 (2.8m)	■ Camel #43
77 (70.4m)	■ Yellow #57
	Uncoded background on chickens is white #41 Continental Stitches
	⁄ Black #00 Straight Stitch
	⁄ Beige #39 Straight Stitch
	⁄ White #41 (2-ply) Straight Stitch
	⁄ White #41 (1-ply) Straight Stitch
	⁄ Yellow #57 Straight Stitch
	#3 Pearl Cotton
9 (8.3m)	⁄ Black Backstitch
	#5 Pearl Cotton
3 (2.8m)	⁄ Black Backstitch Straight Stitch and Straight Stitch
Color numbers given are for Uniek Needloft plastic canvas yarn.	

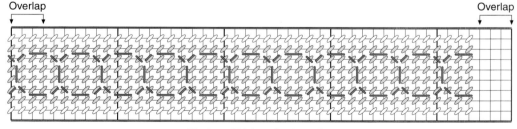

Overlap   Overlap

Kitchen Chicken Shaker Ring
47 holes x 9 holes
Cut 2 from clear

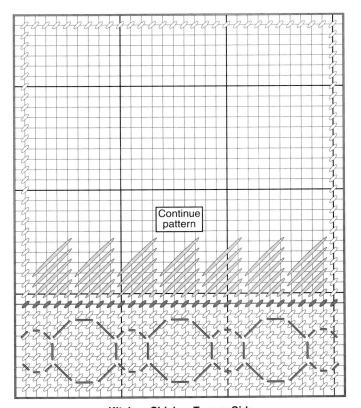

Whipstitch to caddy back

Whipstitch to caddy front

Kitchen Chicken Caddy Base
53 holes x 29 holes
Cut 2 from stiff
Stitch as 1

Continue pattern

Kitchen Chicken Topper Side
31 holes x 37 holes
Cut 3 from regular
Kitchen Chicken Caddy Back
31 holes x 37 holes
Cut 1 from stiff

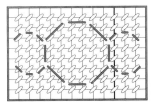

Kitchen Chicken Caddy Side
13 holes x 9 holes
Cut 2 from stiff

COLOR KEY

Yards	Plastic Canvas Yarn
42 (38.4m)	■ Black #00
4 (3.7m)	■ Red #01
1 (1m)	■ Burgundy #03
3 (2.8m)	☐ Eggshell #39
2 (1.9m)	☐ Beige #40
46 (42.1m)	☐ White #41
3 (2.8m)	■ Camel #43
77 (70.4m)	☐ Yellow #57
	Uncoded background on chickens is white #41 Continental Stitches
	✎ Black #00 Straight Stitch
	✎ Beige #39 Straight Stitch
	✎ White #41 (2-ply) Straight Stitch
	✎ White #41 (1-ply) Straight Stitch
	✎ Yellow #57 Straight Stitch
	#3 Pearl Cotton
9 (8.3m)	✎ Black Backstitch
	#5 Pearl Cotton
3 (2.8m)	✎ Black Backstitch Straight Stitch and Straight Stitch

Color numbers given are for Uniek Needloft plastic canvas yarn.

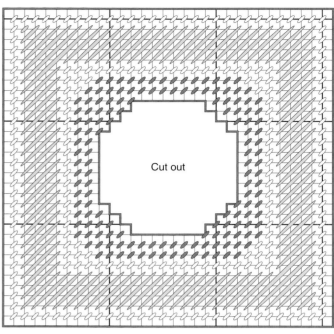

Kitchen Chicken Topper Top
31 holes x 31 holes
Cut 1 from regular

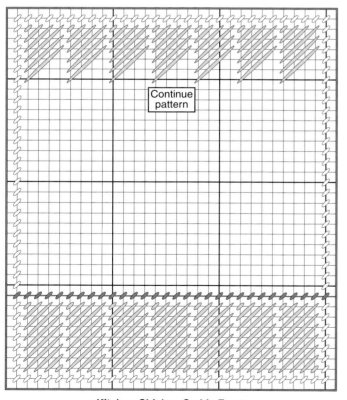

Kitchen Chicken Caddy Front
31 holes x 37 holes
Cut 1 from stiff

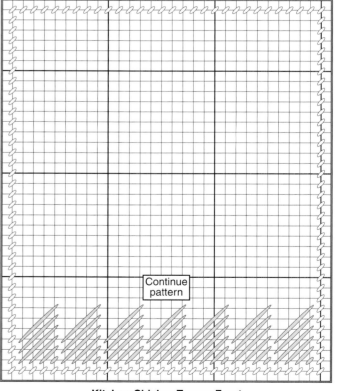

Kitchen Chicken Topper Front
31 holes x 37 holes
Cut 1 from regular

Special Thanks

We would like to acknowledge and thank the following designers whose original work has been published in this collection. We appreciate and value their creativity and dedication to designing quality plastic canvas projects!

Debra Arch
Cool School Tools, Red Hat Style, Regal Cardinal, Sweet Liberty

Angie Arickx
Apple Coffee Can Covers

Janna Britton
Strawberry Dollhouse & Furniture

Ronda Bryce
Apron Napkin Rings, Gone Fishin' Card Holder, Pigs in a Poke Coasters, Sewing Notions Catch-All

Pam Bull
Holiday Tags

Judy Collishaw
Ewes Welcome, Joy, Little Angel Hearts, North Pole Goodie Boxes

Mary T. Cosgrove
Dairy Dudes Fridgie Friends, Noah's Ark Suncatcher, Picnic Guest

Nancy Dorman
Santa Bear Coasters, Summertime Fridgies

Janelle Giese
Beaded Bear Wind Chime, Couch Potato Bag Clip, Halloween Surprise, Kitchen Chicken, Precious Pets' Food Clips, Quilting Bee, Bluebird Songs

Kathleen Hurley
Christmas in Ladybug Land, Plant Poke Buddies

Patricia Klesh
Tiny Treasures

Nancy Knapp
Floral Fantasy Frames, Water Babies

Christina Laws
Best Friend

Lee Lindeman
Kitty Cell Cozy & Key Chain, The Gardener Bunny

Terry Ricioli
Beaded Stocking, Floral Trellis Photo Holder, Grandma's Favorite Chair, Summer Floral Explosion

Deborah Scheblein
Baby Buggy, Buzz on in Door Hanger, Calico Kitty Note Clip

Debbie Tabor
Doggie Welcome, Happy Hound Towel Holder, Patriotic Angel

Laura Victory
Festive Snowman Ornament, Time for Fall Turkey Set

Mary Nell Wall
Sleepy Moon Baby Decor

Michele Wilcox
Ahoy, Matey, Summer Celebration Set, Cute Kitten, Peace on Earth, Topsy-Turvy Cat

Kathy Wirth
Bluebird Welcome, Mini Butterfly Tote

Stitch Guide

Use the following diagrams to expand your plastic canvas stitching skills. For each diagram, bring needle up through canvas at the red number 1 and go back down through the canvas at the red number 2. The second stitch is numbered in green. Always bring needle up through the canvas at odd numbers and take it back down through the canvas at the even numbers.

Background Stitches

The following stitches are used for filling in large areas of canvas. The Continental Stitch is the most commonly used stitch. Other stitches, such as the Condensed Mosaic and Scotch Stitch, fill in large areas of canvas more quickly than the Continental Stitch because their stitches cover a larger area of canvas.

Continental Stitch

Condensed Mosaic

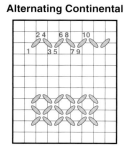

Alternating Continental

Cross Stitch

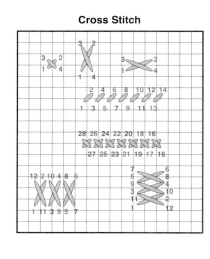

Long Stitch

Scotch Stitch

Slanting Gobelin

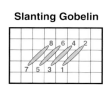

Embroidery Stitches

These stitches are worked on top of a stitched area to add detail to the project. Embroidery stitches are usually worked with one strand of yarn, several strands of pearl cotton or several strands of embroidery floss.

Lattice Stitch

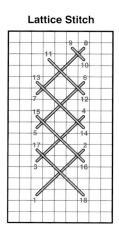

Chain Stitch

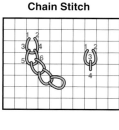

Straight Stitch

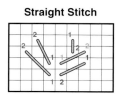

Fly Stitch

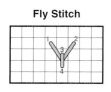

Running Stitch

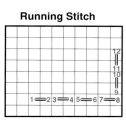

Couching

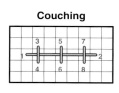

Backstitch

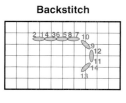

Embroidery Stitches

French Knot

Bring needle up through canvas.

Wrap yarn around needle 2 or 3 times, depending on desired size of knot; take needle back through canvas through same hole.

Lazy Daisy

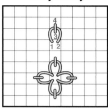

Bring yarn needle up through canvas, then back down in same hole, leaving a small loop.

Then, bring needle up inside loop; take needle back down through canvas on other side of loop.

Loop Stitch or Turkey Loop Stitch

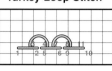

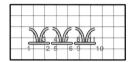

The top diagram shows this stitch left intact. This is an effective stitch for giving a project dimensional hair. The bottom diagram demonstrates the cut loop stitch. Because each stitch is anchored, cutting it will not cause the stitches to come out. A group of cut loop stitches gives a fluffy, soft look and feel to your project.

Specialty Stitches

The following stitches can be worked either on top of a previously stitched area or directly onto the canvas. Like the embroidery stitches, these too add wonderful detail and give your stitching additional interest and texture.

Diamond Eyelet

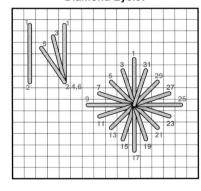

For each stitch, bring needle up at odd numbers around outside and take needle down through canvas at center hole.

Smyrna Cross

Satin Stitches

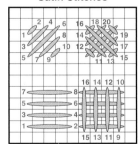

This stitch gives a "padded" look to your work.

Finishing Stitches

Overcast/Whipstitch

Overcasting and Whipstitching are used to finish the outer edges of the canvas. Overcasting is done to finish one edge at a time. Whipstitch is used to stitch two or more pieces of canvas together along on edges. For both Overcasting and Whipstitching, work one stitch in each hole along straight edges and inside corners, and two or three stitches in outside corners.

Lark's Head Knot

The Lark's Head Knot is used for a fringe edge or for attaching a hanging loop.

Buyer's Guide

When looking for a specific material, first check your local craft and retail stores. If you are unable to locate a product locally, contact the manufacturers listed below for the closest retail source in your area or a mail-order source.

Amaco
American Art Clay Co. Inc.
4717 W. 16th St.
Indianapolis, IN 46222-2598
(317) 244-6871
www.amaco.com

Coats & Clark Inc.
Consumer Service
P.O. Box 12229
Greenville, SC 29612-0229
(800) 648-1479
www.coatsandclark.com

Darice
Mail-order source:
Schrock's International
P.O. Box 538
Bolivar, OH 44612
(330) 874-3700

DMC Corp.
Hackensack Ave., Bldg. 10A
South Kearny, NJ 07032-4688
(800) 275-4117
www.dmc-usa.com

Duncan Enterprises
5673 E. Shields Ave.
Fresno, CA 93727
(800) 438-6226
www.duncancrafts.com

Jesse James & Co. Inc.
Dress It Up Buttons
Distributor:
Shelly's Buttons & More
153 Regency Dr.
Uniontown, PA 15401
(888) 811-7441
ww.shellysbuttonandmore.com

Kreinik Mfg. Co. Inc.
3106 Lord Baltimore Dr. #101
Baltimore, MD 21244-2871
(800) 537-2166
www.kreinik.com

Lion Brand Yarn Co.
34 W. 15th St.
New York, NY 10011
(800) 258-9276
www.lionbrand.com

Rainbow Gallery
7412 Fulton Ave., #5
North Hollywood, CA 91605
(818) 982-4496
www.rainbowgallery.com

Spinrite Inc.
P.O. Box 435
Lockport, NY 14094-0435
(800) 265-2864

Box 40
Listowel, Ontario N4W 3H3
Canada
(519) 291-3780
www.bernat.com

Uniek
Mail-order source:
Annie's Attic
1 Annie Ln.
Big Sandy, TX 75755
(800) 582-6643
www.anniesattic.com